PRINCE
COMPANION

PROJECT ASSURANCE
FUNCTION

David E Marsh

London: The Stationery Office

ISBN – 0117022977

Printed in the United Kingdom for The Stationery Office
J52673 C8 7/98 9385 8475

*This book is dedicated to my children
Jenni and Steven*

May all their projects be a success.

Project Assurance Function

CONTENTS

Project Assurance Function

INTRODUCTION TO THE PRINCE *COMPANION*

The PRINCE Method

The use of structured project management methods is not new.

Most organisations and computer consultancies have found that to successfully control the development of a project a structured approach to the management is essential.

PRINCE was developed in 1988/89 as the result of an initiative sponsored by the Central Computer and Telecommunication Agency to update the PROMPT II method which had been used in UK Government departments for over seven years. It was further enhanced in 1996 to the current version of the method PRINCE V2.

PRINCE Version 2 was designed with the following concepts in mind:

1   To ensure that projects were directed to providing business solutions.
2   To be applicable to all types of projects.
3   To ensure that senior management can control a project.
4   To ensure that the project is planned and controlled by the Project Team.
5   That the organisation is totally involved in the project's development.

The major new features in PRINCE Version 2 are:

1   The introduction of a business driven process approach to the project management of a project.
2   The introduction of a project Start Up process.
3   A greater focus on the business justification elements of the project.

Project Assurance Function

1

4   The introduction of new terms for some of the roles in the organisation structure.
5   The introduction of the role of Project Support and Team Manager.

The PRINCE method and its supporting processes are fully described in the manual published by The Stationery Office.

The PRINCE Version 2 method uses a number of terms in a specific way.

The most important of these are:

Product, deliverable or outcome:
Something which represents a completed activity or piece of work e.g. a document, or piece of a computer program, or screen design, installation of a washing machine, etc.

Work Package:
Something which represents a significant block, or set of related activities or Work Packages and or Products e.g. the initial design of the building, a set of cost or materials estimates receipt of Building Permission, registering a company with Companies House.

Senior User/*Customer*:
The owner of the project - the commissioner or sponsor of the project and normally responsible for the funds used to complete the project.

User/*Customer*:
The members of the organisation who will use the Work Packages and or Products supplied by the project.

Project Assurance Function

Specialist Supplier:
The members of the team who are supplying the Work Packages and or Products required to complete the project. This Specialist Supplier can be internal or external to the organisation.

Project Management Team:
This collective term is used in the *PRINCE Companions* to describe the Project Board, Project Manager, Team Manager/s, members of the Project Assurance and Project Support Function.

Project Team:
This collective term is used in the *PRINCE Companions* to describe all the staff - including those from the Specialist Supplier and User/*Customer* communities who are allocated to the development and review of the project's Work Packages and or Products.

USING THE *COMPANION*

For the members of a PRINCE Project Management Team there is a *Companion* which is organised as follows:

1   A checklist of the tasks to be done by at specific times during the project.

2   Detailed guidance notes on the what/who/why of each of the tasks contained in the checklist.

   [Note: It is expected that the use of the detailed notes will decrease as you increase your level of skill and knowledge of PRINCE.]

3   Examples of the various forms, documents, agendas, reports needed.

Project Assurance Function

This *Companion* cannot give all the story.

The development of an infrastructure to support PRINCE must be specific to each organisation.
Therefore this *Companion* cannot explain the fine detail of how you find, for example, the Product Descriptions used in previous projects.
The *Companion* does tell you, however, WHEN and WHY you should find them and WHO to ask.

The information contained in this *Companion* has proved essential when implementing PRINCE.

The strength of the PRINCE method is that it can be adapted to a wide range of projects, organisations and environments. These *Companions* will provide PRACTICAL advice and help in all situations.

Project Assurance Function

4

1. INTRODUCTION TO PRINCE

The PRINCE Methodology (body of methods) provides a framework of guidance to assist in undertaking the various processes involved in project management, particularly the organisation, planning, and control of a project. Fundamental to the PRINCE approach is a focus on Work Packages and or Products - firstly on those Products that are required to manage the project, secondly on those that are required to achieve the ultimate objective of the project, and thirdly on those that relate to the management of quality in the project. These three types of Products are referred to in PRINCE as Management, Specialist and Quality Products.

Within PRINCE there are a series of Components or frameworks to support the project management processes. These components include:

- an organisation structure;
- sets of plans;
- a range of control mechanisms;
- an approach to Quality Management;
- an approach to Configuration Management.
- an approach to Risk Management

1.1 Implementing PRINCE

To implement PRINCE successfully into a particular organisation it is necessary to tune the method and to develop supporting project management systems.

This can only be accomplished successfully if the organisation respects the following advice:

Project Assurance Function

1 Take the method to the project/organisation, NOT put your project/organisation through the method.
2 Never remove any functions or responsibilities, move them, do not ignore them.
3 More projects fail through lack of CONTROL than bad planning.
4 It is possible to plan the project into paralysis.

PLAN to the level you can control

5 Monitor the success of your tuning of the method and amend it if needed.

Most organisations use an external consultancy to help them implement PRINCE.

Typically consultants found that companies needed specific guidance for each of the major PRINCE roles. These *Companions* are the result of much of this work.

1.2 The Structure Of PRINCE

The official PRINCE manual is divided into five sections:

- Introduction;
- Components;
- Processes;
- Techniques;
- Appendices.

Most organisations adopting PRINCE find that the manual does not explain what the members of a PRINCE Project Management Team should do at a particular point.

Project Assurance Function

These *Companions* have been specifically developed and designed to address this problem.

1.2.1 The components of PRINCE: ORGANISATION

PRINCE advocates a particular organisation structure in order to achieve success in a project and in its management. The structure assumes that the project environment will be that of a User/*Customer*/Specialist Supplier (or Provider) relationship. These separate parties may be part of the same corporate body or may be entirely independent of each other.

The 'User/*Customer*' will specify the desired outcome and pay for the project and the (prime) 'Specialist Supplier' will provide the resources and skills to achieve the desired outcome.

Projects need direction, management, control, and communication, and the flexible approach in PRINCE enables these requirements to be met in any type of project environment.

The flexibility is achieved through a framework of defined *roles* rather than *jobs*. It is then possible to allocate, share, divide, or combine roles according to the needs of the particular project. The particular project-specific structure will be determined by considering who is affected by the project and its outcome. For example:

- the business;
- internal and/or external User/*Customer*s;
- internal and/or external Suppliers or specialists;
- the working environment (including staff associations, unions etc.);
- a wider Programme of which the project is part.

Project Assurance Function

The structure has four layers - the direction of the project, its day-to-day management, team management, and the working level at which Work Packages and or Products are created. The PRINCE Project Management Team comprising a Project Board, a Project Manager, a Team Manager address the first three levels. An independent Project Assurance Function is also a vital component.

Project Board

The PRINCE approach requires a minimum of two people to fulfill the role of a Project Board. The Board members are usually appointed by Corporate or Programme Management.

They represent the Business, User/*Customer*, and the Specialist Supplier/Provider interests of the particular environment in which the project exists.

Jointly they are responsible for the Project and accountable for its success. They have authority within the remit of the Project Mandate set by Corporate or Programme Management and must provide overall direction and management.

The *Business* considerations are concerned with the project meeting a business need and providing value for money.

The *User/Customer* interest is in specifying a desired outcome and being able to use the final Product of the project or ensuring that there is no adverse impact from the outcome of the project.

The *Specialist Supplier/Provider* interest is in the provision of the necessary skilled resources and their conformance to any defined standards in order to create the desired outcome.

Project Assurance Function

The defined responsibilities and associated tasks (documented) of a Project Board relate to:

- ensuring ownership of the project;
- approving the appointment and responsibilities of the Project Manager and any persons assigned to the Project Assurance Function;
- determining whether the project is, or continues to be, worthwhile;
- approving plans and authorising the project to proceed;
- ensuring that the project is adequately resourced to implement the approved plans;
- formally accepting the Project Management Products of the project throughout its existence and at its closure.

The Project Board is actively involved at the beginning of the project, as it progresses, and in formally closing it down at the end. They own the PRINCE process 'Directing a Project' which addresses the details of their activities and tasks.

Project Manager

The role of Project Manager is defined, documented, and assigned to someone who is then responsible to the Project Board for the day-to-day management of the project on their behalf.

The Project Board will delegate authority to the Project Manager so that decisions which need to be made, but which will impact upon the approved timescales and expenditure plans, can nevertheless be made without referral, but within pre-defined constraints. This is termed 'Tolerance'.

Project Assurance Function

9

The Project Manager's key responsibilities are to ensure that the project produces the required Work Packages and or Products to the specified standard of quality within the set time and cost constraints and that the result can achieve the benefits defined in the Project Initiation Document.

The Project Manager's tasks are principally in the areas of:

- resource allocation and management;
- preparation of plans;
- identification and management of risks;
- progress monitoring and reporting;
- liaison with the Project Board, the Project Assurance Function and where the project is part of a Programme, the Business Change Manager.

Team Manager

The allocation of this role to an individual other than the Project Manager is optional. A Team Manager takes direction from and reports to the Project Manager. The role is defined, documented, and assigned to an individual where it will be beneficial to delegate the authority for the Production of particular Work Packages and or Products and for the management of the specialist skills producing the Work Packages and or Products. Factors influencing the decision to separately assign the role are:

- the size of the project;
- the particular specialist skills or knowledge required;
- geographical location of team members;
- Project Board preferences.

Project Assurance Function

The Team Manager's tasks are principally in the areas of:

- preparation of plans for the team;
- progress monitoring and reporting;
- attending Checkpoint and team control meetings;
- liaison with the Project Assurance Function;
- the Project Issue procedure.

Project Assurance

In PRINCE project assurance is internal and external. Responsibility for internal project assurance rests with the Project Board. ***The assurance roles may or may not be delegated and could be assigned to one or more individuals but the Project Board must retain RESPONSIBILITY for Project Assurance***. Those fulfilling these roles must remain independent of the Project Manager. Their prime function is to give independent assurance to the Project Board that :

- the project and its plans are viable;
- the project Work Packages and or Products are acceptable;
- the project conforms to any appropriate standards;
- the scope of the project is not 'creeping';
- focus on business needs is maintained;
- internal and external communications are working;
- the needs of special interests (e.g. security) are being met;
- User/*Customer* needs are being met;
- business risks are under control;
- consistency with the overall Programme or company strategy is maintained.

Project Assurance Function

Ensuring that the project conforms to BS ISO EN standards is an example of external assurance.

Project Support

Formal arrangements for Project Support are optional and will be determined by the particular needs of the project and the Project Manager. Project Support could be required in the form of administrative services, and advice or guidance, and could be available to more than one project.

Where it is formalised and a Project Support Office is set up it can capture and retain project progress information from which it can provide data for estimating and planning and from which the lessons to be learned from past project experiences can be collated and promulgated.

It can become a source of expertise in planning, in the application of PRINCE and in the use of software support tools. It may also encompass a Configuration Management function.

1.2.2   The components of PRINCE: PLANNING

Plans are vital to the success of a project and must contain a range of information to confirm that the objectives of the project and its plans are achievable. The objectives of the plan are to define how the work of the project will be approached, when it will be undertaken, who will perform the tasks and how much it will all cost.

Project Assurance Function

In PRINCE plans are a statement of the:

- Work Packages and or Products required;
- necessary activities to produce the Work Packages and or Products;
- timing of those activities;
- activities necessary to validate Product quality;
- resources and particular skills required;
- dependencies between activities and external dependencies;
- facilities required for the project;
- risks identified and the countermeasures proposed.

These comprehensive plans then become the basis of a commitment to their implementation and provide a means of communicating information about the project.

Additional narrative information is required to explain:

- the scope and coverage of the plans
- how the plan will be implemented;
- the monitoring, control, and reporting arrangements;
- any assumptions that underpin the plan;
- any pre-requisites;
- the assessment of risks that threaten the plan.

Levels of plan

It is impossible to plan the entire duration of a project in detail from the start yet detailed plans are required in order to allocate work and to control and monitor its progress. Therefore different levels of plan (in terms of their scope and detail) are necessary.

Project Assurance Function

13

In PRINCE this is achieved by the initial production of a Project Level Plan, and a Stage Level Plan in more detail for the first of its Stages. Thereafter towards the end of each Stage, plans are required to be prepared in more detail for the subsequent Stage at which time also the validity of any assumptions made initially can be confirmed and the analysis of risks reassessed.

Within each Stage lower level plans may be required, perhaps at the Team Level for discrete teams who are implementing different aspects of the Stage Plan. In addition to these Project Plans in some projects it may be necessary to provide further levels of plans perhaps in the form of Checklists etc.

The Project Plan

The Project Plan provides a total overview of the project from start to finish and is therefore likely to be very approximate in terms of timescales and costs particularly towards the end of the planned project lifecycle. It identifies the key Work Packages and or Products, the major resource requirements and costs, and Stage boundaries.

Once accepted and approved for implementation it will be baselined and retained for future comparison with actual progress. Stage by Stage it should be reviewed and revised in the light of progress made, any agreed changes affecting the project, and any revision of forecasts.

The Stage Plan

The Stage Plan provides a basis for day-to-day control and monitoring.

Project Assurance Function

To achieve that control, and to facilitate the allocation of work to the planned available resources, the Stage Plan shows the major elements of the Project Plan for the Stage broken down to whatever increased level of detail is required.

It will often be created from the plans produced by the Specialist teams or Suppliers for the accomplishment of their own tasks and will provide an overall view of the resource requirements, timings, and interdependencies in the work of the Stage. Successive Stage Plans will also take into account the experience and knowledge gained in previous Stages and the implications of past performance for the future estimating and planning.

The Team Plan

These are optional but would be appropriate where there is a Team Management role allocated or where the Stage Plan has been created from the different Teams' separate plans especially when a variety of discrete skills may be involved.

The Exception Plan

This is created at the behest of the Project Board after it is has been predicted in an Exception Report that a plan will not be able to be implemented within the agreed Tolerances. The Exception Plan will most often be created to replace the current Stage Plan but could replace a Project Plan if that were appropriate. It will have the same format as the plan it replaces but it will be accompanied by additional text which will include the following information extracted from the Exception Report:

- the cause of the deviation;
- the options open;

Project Assurance Function

- the likely consequences of taking no action;
- a recommendation from the Project Manager;
- impact on the Project Plan (if a lower level Exception Plan), the Business Case, and the risks.

Steps in planning

PRINCE provides a planning framework to enable the logical sequence of project work to be shown. It is applicable to any project and begins with the identification of all the Work Packages and or Products required to comprise the ultimate end-Product of the project and the creation of Product Breakdown Structure Diagrams. These will also depict those Products required to facilitate project management (Management Products), and those required during the processes of Quality Management (Quality Products) and to support the management and control of the plan.

Secondly, Product Descriptions are part of the Work Packages and define the constituent Products in terms of :

- Product title;
- purpose (what purpose the Product fulfills, whether it is a means to an end or an end in itself);
- composition (the components of the Product);
- derivation (the source(s) from which this Product is derived a design based on a specification, a Product purchased from a Supplier, or a Product obtained from another section or team);
- format and presentation (a standard appearance to which the Product must conform);
- allocated to (who has to produce the Product);
- Quality Criteria (the specification, standards or other measurements against which the Product will be inspected);
- type of quality check required;

Project Assurance Function

16

- people or skills required for reviewing/testing/approving the Product.

Thirdly a Product Flow Diagram can be derived from the Product Breakdown Structure to depict the sequence of development and to identify dependencies on any Work Packages and or Products outside the scope of the plan.

Planning the necessary activities to produce the Work Packages and or Products can then be undertaken, along with determining the appropriate resource requirements and the costs that will therefore be incurred. Finally the specific plan documents and diagrams are produced along with supporting explanatory narrative including information about:

- constraints;
- external dependencies;
- assumptions made;
- risks and countermeasures.

1.2.3 The components of PRINCE: CONTROLS

Levels of control

The PRINCE formal control mechanisms operate at the various levels in the project and are mostly event-driven. At Project Board level the concept of 'management by exception' applies. The specific control mechanisms that involve the Project Board are:

- Project Initiation;
- End-Stage Assessment and Reports;
- Highlight Reports;

Project Assurance Function

17

- Exception Reports;
- Mid-Stage Assessments;
- End of Project Reports.

At the Project Manager level day to day control is exercised, specifically through Work Package Authorisation and Checkpoints through which the Teams report back on progress.

Types of control

PRINCE Controls enable the start of a project, its progress, and its closure to be controlled. The controlled start involves a number of Start-Up Processes including planning an Initiation Stage during which a Project Plan will be prepared, identifying the various Stages of the project lifecycle. The Initiation Stage concludes with the production of a Project Initiation Document (PID).

Controls during the progress of the project are intended to ensure that it remains aligned to the PID and the current Stage Plan. The components are:
- Tolerance (limited authority to deviate from the timescales and costs in the plan);
- Product Descriptions (specifications of Product content and quality);
- Work Package Authorisation (authority to produce specific Work Packages and or Products);
- Quality Control (checking or reviewing Product quality);
- Project Issues (a means of addressing deviations from specifications, questions, or change requests);
- Change Control (procedures to maintain control over requested or required changes);

Project Assurance Function

18

- Risk Logs (facilitating review of identified risks, their analysis, status and associated countermeasures);
- Checkpoints (a review of what is and what is not going according to plan, the information being documented for the Project Manager);
- Highlight Report (a periodic report from the Project Manager to the Project Board);
- Exception Report (a warning from the Project Manager to the Project Board forecasting a deviation from the Stage or Project Plan exceeding the Tolerance);
- End-Stage Report (an opportunity for the Project Board to review the project and decide whether or not to authorise progress to the next Stage);
- End-Stage Assessment (from the Project Manager to the Project Board informing them of the results of the work of the Stage);
- Mid-Stage Assessment (a meeting of the Project Manager and the Project Board, following an Exception Report, at which the Project Manager presents an Exception Plan for approval).

The controlled close of a project involves checking that all the intended Work Packages and or Products have been delivered and accepted, ensuring that the Product can be used and supported, ensuring that any lessons learned are passed on, and ensuring that a check will be made to confirm that the benefits claimed in the Business Case have actually been achieved.

The specific components are:

- End Product Notification (a formal notice to providers of resources or services that the project is ending);
- End-Project Report (similar to an End-Stage Report but for the whole project);

Project Assurance Function

19

- Follow-On Action Recommendations (documenting any unfinished work so that it can be formally redirected);
- Lessons Learned Report (capturing any useful lessons for dissemination to others);
- Plan for a Post Implementation Review (identifying when and how achievement of benefits will be measured).

1.2.4 The components of PRINCE: STAGES

Stages are sub-divisions of the project for management and control purposes. Work is authorised one Stage at a time and resources are committed for that period only. There is an opportunity at the end of each Stage to formally review the project and confirm (or otherwise) its continued viability before further commitment to it.

Every project requires at least two Stages - Initiation and the rest of the project - but the specific needs of a particular project will dictate the precise number necessary.

Breaking the work down into Stages aids more accurate planning and estimating. Defining the Stages is therefore achieved by deciding how far ahead it is sensible or possible to plan and determining at what points the key decisions will need to be made within the project. A balance will need to be struck between having too many short Stages and too few long ones.

1.2.5 The components of PRINCE: THE MANAGEMENT OF RISK

In PRINCE risk is defined as "the chance of exposure to the adverse consequences of future events".

Project Assurance Function

Given that projects are generally helping to bring about change, usually unique one-off discrete pieces of work to be achieved within time and cost constraints, they are inherently risky.

Projects may often be large and complex as well as novel or unusual. Nevertheless there are specific risks that affect all projects regardless of their size and nature e.g. Business Risks such as the viability of the Business Case and the impact the project may have on the Business, and Project Risks such as management, organisation, and resourcing issues.

Management of risk is therefore a key aspect of the Project Manager's and the Project Board's role. The Project Board should be particularly aware of risks that are external to the project but pose a threat to it. Managing risk involves:

Risk Analysis:

- Risk Identification;
- Risk Estimation;
- Risk Evaluation;

Risk Management:

- Planning;
- Resourcing;
- Controlling;
- Monitoring.

The possible actions that can be taken are:

- prevention - countermeasures to prevent occurrence or impact of occurrence on the project;
- reduction - reducing the likelihood or limiting the impact to acceptable levels;

Project Assurance Function

21

- transference - passing the risk to a third party;
- contingency - plans ready for implementation when the risk occurs;
- acceptance - where countermeasures are disproportionately expensive or there is doubt that the risk will occur.

1.2.6 The components of PRINCE: QUALITY

PRINCE bases its guidance on the ISO 8402 definition of quality which relates it to fitness for purpose and the satisfaction of identified needs. Quality Management is the process of ensuring that the User/*Customer*s' expectations of quality are met and in PRINCE managing quality in a project includes:

- ensuring that documented systems and procedures exist and are being followed (quality assurance);
- that all planning takes account of activity and resource requirements associated with Quality Management (Quality Planning);
- that quality is checked by formally reviewing Work Packages and or Products to ensure that their Quality Criteria are met and that they are fit for their purpose (quality control).

The implementation of the PRINCE concept of Product Descriptions is crucial to successful Quality Management in a project environment.

Project Assurance Function

1.2.7 The components of PRINCE: CONFIGURATION MANAGEMENT

Configuration Management is required in a project to identify, track, and protect project Work Packages and or Products. PRINCE advocates a system within the project for:-

- identifying Configuration Items and maintaining description records;
- controlling Configuration Items , their filing, storage, and distribution;
- handling any changes necessary or requested;
- accounting for Configuration Items and tracking changes in their status;
- conducting audits or reviews of Configuration Items and the system.

Control of change and the ability to identify and control different versions of a configuration item is crucial. Control of change involves:

- impact assessment;
- assessing relative importance;
- establishing costs;
- management judgment and decision-making.

1.3 Benefits Of Using PRINCE

PRINCE is a flexible approach in that its concepts can be applied and scaled down (or up) according to the size, complexity, perceived degree of risk, scope, and nature of the particular project, I.T. or non-I.T.

Project Assurance Function

It is based on principles that are universally applicable to projects and their successful management. The PRINCE framework offers guidance on <u>what</u> must be done and <u>why</u>, in order to achieve a more successful outcome than may otherwise be achieved without adoption of any structured approach. The <u>how</u> is left largely to those responsible for and managing the project. They must therefore apply the concepts on the basis of a sound understanding of the approach and with discretion, judgment, common sense, and awareness of the level of risk.

Little is mandatory or prescriptive and even the formal mechanisms are simple and need not be bureaucratic. The PRINCE User/*Customer* has a free hand to determine the nature of any documentation that is recommended. No forms are included in the official manuals though there is guidance on what should be recorded and documented.

In the PRINCE approach the emphasis is on:

- formally initiating a project;
- formally closing it down;
- focusing throughout on Work Packages and or Products and their quality;
- documenting the various roles, responsibilities and tasks;
- combining roles where appropriate;
- developing a disciplined approach to planning, monitoring, control, and risk analysis and management.

Wise use of PRINCE in implementing the above has proved to be a powerful force in improving the standard of effective project management.

Project Assurance Function

2. INTRODUCTION TO THE PROJECT ASSURANCE FUNCTION

The responsibility for Project Assurance rests with the Project Board. In some projects they also perform the detailed tasks and processes required to meet that responsibility - however the most common situation is for them to delegate part of that role to other members of staff.

This delegation is needed because of the time and other constraints that may exist on them or they may well not have the sufficient detailed knowledge of some of the critical assurance issues that need to be addressed.

When this delegation occurs the Project Assurance Function needs to be carried out by staff who have a wide range of skills and experience. The typical role (as defined in the PRINCE manual) will need to be tuned to reflect the environment in which the project is undertaken, the working relationship and arrangements with the Project Board, the Project Manager, and the supporting project management systems and procedures.

Of all the PRINCE roles the responsibilities of Project Assurance - as described in the PRINCE Manual - are the most likely to require amendment. This is because of two factors.

The first of these is that the Project Board has overall responsibility for Project Assurance and therefore members of staff are appointed to provide those aspects of project assurance that the Project Board have decided to delegate to them. The amount and level of this delegation will therefore depend on the experience of the members of the Project Board and the time or other resources they can commit to this assurance function.

Project Assurance Function

The second factor concerns the structure of the members of staff who will perform the delegated Project Assurance Function; in that it may mirror the Project Board structure by having 3 members of staff allocated to look after the User/*Customer*, Specialist Supplier and Business aspects and may be staffed by part time or full time staff, with one or more members of staff allocated to each aspect.

The tuning of the role and responsibilities can be substantial. Typically, however, the major functions of the Project Assurance Function - assurance to the Project Board - is usually done by the same group of people throughout the project.

The decision on what the Project Assurance Function structure should be is made during the design of the Project Management Team during the Set Up Stage of the project.

PROJECT ASSURANCE FUNCTION

Prime Responsibility

To provide assurance to the Project Board that the Business, User/*Customer* and Specialist Supplier aspects of the project are being managed in accordance with the agreed plans and strategies.

Main Tasks

Monitor and report to the Project Board any User/*Customer*, Business and Specialist Supplier problems which arise during the project's realisation.

Project Assurance Function

User/*Customer* Aspects Role

- ensure that adequate liaison arrangements exist between the User/*Customer* and the Supplier;
- ensure the User/*Customer* needs and expectations are being effectively managed and will be met by the project's realisation;
- ensure that the "right" people in the organisation are being involved in its realisation;
- ensure that the realisation of the Communication Strategy has ensured that the external and internal communications are working satisfactorily;
- monitor all Project Issues and assist with assessment of their impact;
  ensure that the impact of any request for change is understood and accepted by the User/*Customer*;

Business Aspects Role

- ensure that risks to the project are identified, controlled, contained or eliminated;
- ensure that the Business Case and Benefits Realisation Plan are up to date and the project is within the scope of these documents;
- ensure that regularly the value for money aspects of the solution proposed to meet the projects requirements are reviewed;
- ensure that the project remains within the relevant programme or company strategy;
- ensure that the project remains viable as compared to the Business Case;
- ensure the scope of the project is not expanding or "creeping";
- ensure the focus on the business needs of the project is maintained;
- ensure that the realisation of the Communication Strategy has ensured that the external and internal communications are working satisfactorily;

Project Assurance Function

27

- monitor all Project Issues and assist with assessment of their impact;
- ensure that the impact of any request for change is understood and accepted by the User/*Customer* community;

Specialist Supplier Aspects Role
- Ensure that the project realisation is providing an acceptable solution to the project's requirements;
- Ensure that the Specialist Supplier is using appropriate standards and methods of development;
- Ensure that requirements of any relevant legislation or codes of practice are being identified and catered for in the project realisation;
- Ensure any specialist requirements such as security, recovery or resilience have been identified and are being catered for;
- Ensure that any Products developed during the project's realisation adhere to any specified quality assurance standards;
- ensure that the realisation of the Communication Strategy has ensured that the external and internal communications are working satisfactorily;
- monitor all Project Issues and assist with assessment of their impact;
- ensure that the impact of any request for change is understood and accepted by the Specialist Supplier community;

Required Knowledge and Experience
- Good working knowledge of PRINCE;
- Good working knowledge of the Products that will be developed during the project's realisation;
- Good working knowledge of User/*Customer* departments operations and how they will be affected by the project;

Project Assurance Function

- Good working knowledge of the development and updating of a Business Case and a Benefits Realisation Plan;
- An understanding of the human factors necessary for ensuring the usability of the end Products of the project;
- Capable of establishing good communications between the User/*Customer*s and the Project Team.

3. STARTING UP A PROJECT

3.1 Objectives of the Process

This is in effect the first process in the management of a project. This process contains two steps. The first is where the Project Board and other members of the Project Management Team are appointed. Thus this part of the process is pre-project. The second part of the process is the start of the project. This second part of the process results in the approval of the Project Mandate and Brief for the project. (This is because in PRINCE V2 before a project starts it is vital that there is a mandate for the project and its outcomes.)

In organisations that utilise Programme Management this mandate may come from the Programme Executive.

The objectives of the process are to ensure that:

- responsibility for the project is defined, someone is authorised to direct the work of the project, and there is a Project Management Team for the project;

- there is a basic business requirement for the project (so that the organisation can answer the question "Do we have a project?") and a Project Mandate and Brief has been produced and agreed;

- before the project starts a plan for the Project Initiation Stage has been developed.

Without these elements being in place the organisation cannot ensure that the project starts within a managed and controlled framework.

Project Assurance Function

3.2 Description of the Process

The level of management or committee or board in an organisation (referred to in this document as the Project Commissioning Authority (PCA) who are responsible for commissioning projects must identify who is to be the Executive Member of the Project Board. The Executive Member of the Project Board and or other relevant people then select the Project Manager.

[Note: The identification of the reason for the project and the project commissioning process and the procedures are outside the scope of this document.]

This PCA must provide the Executive Member of the Project Board with sufficient information to enable them and the Project Manager to develop the Project Brief which will be submitted back to the PCA for their final approval before the project is initiated. This information may come from a feasibility or other type of study or a section of a Programme Blueprint - or even 'the back of an envelope!'

This process may be assisted by, or even organised by, a Project or Programme Support Office if the organisation has one.

The Project Board Executive Member and the Project Manager, with input from other relevant members of the organisation, design the Project Management Team and appoint the initial members.

The appointment of the other members of the Project Board (the Senior User/*Customer*, Senior Supplier) and the definition and agreement of their respective roles is the responsibility of the Executive Member assisted by the Project Manager.

Project Assurance Function

The Executive Member, supported if necessary by the rest of the Board, may appoint the Project Manager and also define and agree the role and responsibilities of the appointee.

3.3   Outputs to be Produced by this Process

- SU 1A   Project Board - Executive Member - Appointment

- SU1B   Project Manager - Appointment

- SU2   Project Management Team Design

- SU3   Project Management Team Appointment

- SU4   Project Brief

- SU5   Method of Approach Design

- SU 6   Initiation Stage Plan

Project Assurance Function

3.4 Checklist

A   Ensure you understand your role and responsibilities, in particular your involvement in the development of:

- Project and Stage Plans;
- Product Descriptions and Quality Criteria;
- Quality Reviews;
- The Business Case;
- Risk Assessment.

B   If you are not a full time member of the Project Management Team, ensure your existing organisational responsibilities have been reviewed to take account of your new duties.

C   Establish how you will liaise, communicate and report to the Project Board and the other parts of the organisation.

D   Ensure you have a job description and that it has been approved by the Project Board.

E   Ensure you have access to the following documents:

- Background to the project, Project Mandate, Project Brief, Feasibility Study, Business Case;
- Product Descriptions from other projects;
- any earlier statements of User/*Customer* Requirements.

ADDITIONAL CHECKLIST IF TAKING OVER THE ROLE DURING THE PROJECT

F   Familiarise yourself with the project filing system.

Project Assurance Function

G   The new member of staff assigned to a role in the Project Assurance Function should be introduced to all members of the Project Management Team who are associated with the project.

H   The outgoing member of staff who had been allocated to a role in the Project Assurance Function should prepare a Handover Report which details:

- successes and failures noted so far;
- key areas for the project;
- where to find people/documents.

I   The outgoing member of staff should advise you on how to re-organise your existing duties.

J   The relevant member of the Project Board and the remainder of the members of staff who have a role in the Project Assurance Function must be advised of the changeover and it is advisable to hold a meeting with the Project Team to notify them of the handover.

Project Assurance Function

3.5   Guidance Notes

A   It is essential to have had some formal training in PRINCE before accepting your role. This training should include:

- the philosophy of PRINCE;
- your role in the project;
- the PRINCE organisation structure and the roles;
- how to develop Product Descriptions and Quality Criteria;
- how to act as a reviewer at Quality Reviews;
- how to contribute as a member of the Project Assurance Function in the creation of a Project and Stage Plan.

You can usually obtain advice about the availability/sources of training from the organisation's PRINCE Co-ordinator or Project Support Office. You will need to allow for either three or five days training (depending on your previous project experience).

i)   Your role in the Project Assurance Function in the production of Project and Stage Plans will be determined by:

- the existence of a Project Support Office;
- the way the organisation has implemented PRINCE;
- the relative skills and experience of the Project Manager;
- the size, novelty and complexity of the project.

The Project Assurance Function will be involved in identifying those Products where members of staff (external to the Project Team) should attend as Reviewers and who should accept the Products which have been developed.

Project Assurance Function

35

The members of staff allocated to a role in the Project Assurance Function must also ensure that the necessary Products have been included in the plan. The Project Manager will consult with the members of the Project Assurance Function as to which specific staff are required to assist in the project's realisation.

ii) As with the Project Plans the exact role of the members of the Project Assurance Function in the development and agreement of Product Descriptions and Quality Criteria will be determined by:

- the existence of a Project Support Office;
- the existence of a library of previous Product Descriptions or departmental standards;
- the way the organisation has implemented PRINCE;
- the relative skills and experience of the Project Manager;
- the size, novelty and complexity of the project.

A typical approach when developing Product Descriptions for a project is for Project Manager or Project Support Assistant (or Office) to identify any from previous projects which any may be useful in this project. The members of the Project Assurance Function comment on those that are relevant to their delegated area of authority.

They must pay particular attention to the Quality Criteria to ensure they are realistic and can be practically applied and used.

These are discussed with the Project Manager who will then complete the process of developing and agreeing them for the project.

iii) The role of the members of the Project Assurance Function in Quality Reviews will depend on:

- the existence of a separate quality department;
- the types of reviews that are envisaged for the Products;
- the number of User/*Customer* areas affected by the project's Products.

It may be that the members of the Project Assurance Function have the correct level of knowledge and time available to act as Reviewer for some or all of the Products requiring User/*Customer* assurance. But it is equally valuable for the members of the Project Assurance Function to identify the appropriate members of staff from the organisation who should be invited to a review.

iv) The role of the members of the Project Assurance Function in the production and updating of the Business Case will depend on:

- the existence of a separate department to deal with this aspect of the project's management;
- the type of Business Case that the organisation requires (Full or just a summary of costs and benefits);
- the importance of the Business Case to the commissioning and continuance of the project;

v) The role of the members of the Project Assurance Function in Risk Assessment:

- the existence of a Project or Programme Support Office;
- the types of Risk Assessment that is used - Qualitative or Quantitative;

Project Assurance Function

- the existence and use of a Risk register in that organisation.

B   The role of a member of the Project Assurance Function will involve demands on your time. It is sometimes a full time job, so it is important that you do assess the amount of time you will need to have available and ensure that you review your other commitments and duties.

The members of the Project Assurance Function will have to deal with peaks of work. These occur:

- at the start and end of each Stage;
- when you are enhancing your existing skills or undergoing training;
- if problems occur i.e. Project Issues.

It is recommended that you discuss this with the member of the Project Board you are responsible to and enlist their help in convincing your own Line or Resource Manager that your existing workload needs to be reassessed to take account of these additional duties.

C   It is important that you establish good communication links with other parts of the organisation to ensure that they are involved in the project so it becomes the organisation's project rather than solely the province of the Project Team.

You will need to identify:

- who will need updates/reports on the progress of the project;
- the format and content of those reports;

Project Assurance Function

- what things you can communicate, and to whom, without the permission of the Project Board and/or Project Manager.(See the recommended Communication Strategy Product).

D   The standard PRINCE role description for the Project Assurance Function is shown in Section 2.

This standard job description will have been tailored by you and the Project and Team Managers to reflect:

- this particular project;
- the location of the other members of the Project Assurance Function;
- the project management support systems that exist;
- the size, complexity and novelty of the project;
- the project development strategy (in particular where the development team is not in-house);
- the type of project e.g. bespoke development, package etc;
- the number of User/*Customer* areas affected;
- the amount of time you have available for the Project Assurance Function role.

E   The members of staff allocated to roles in the Project Assurance Function will need access to all the background information.

The key documents to look for are:

- the Project Mandate and Project Brief for the project;
- any Feasibility, Business Study or other documents which summarise the work that preceded the project.

Project Assurance Function

In addition you should also look for documents which provide:

- information which can be used later when assessing the quality of the projects deliverables;
- a list of any unusual combination of events or data in the area to be covered by the system of work (ready for use in the Work Package or Product Acceptance Tests);
- any description of problems encountered or facilities sought in the Project Brief;
- any description of the User/*Customer* or Specialist Supplier organisation structure;
- any future or proposed changes to the User/*Customer* or Specialist Supplier organisation structure.

F   The Project Filing System may already have been established. It is advisable to familiarise yourself with its components and the contents of each section.

The files that will be of particular interest are:

- Project Management products
- Quality Review Documents
- Project Issues

G   In any project the members of the Project Assurance Function will need to make a wide range of contacts both within the project and in the organisation. The outgoing member of the Project Assurance Function must develop a Handover Report which includes a plan for meeting all the contacts and people with whom the outgoing member of the Project Assurance Function has worked.

Project Assurance Function

H The outgoing member of the Project Assurance Function should in addition to the personal handover/induction prepare a report which explains some of the deductions and conclusions made during the project so far. This will be particularly helpful and provide the new member of the Project Assurance Function with the ability to concentrate on the critical aspects of the project.

Of particular interest would be:

- problems identified and any remedial action commissioned;
- the location of documents the new member of the Project Assurance Function will require;
- a contacts list and telephone numbers with 'pen picture' notes.

I The outgoing member of the Project Assurance Function will have gained a major insight into the amount of work/time required to be effective in this project.

This information is extremely useful to the incoming member of the Project Assurance Function to help ensure that the role is allocated the time needed.

J The outgoing member of the Project Assurance Function will have worked closely with the Project Board.
It is important to have a smooth handover of both responsibility and relationship if the project is to continue to flourish.

The outgoing member of the Project Assurance Function should brief the relevant Project Board member about the change and arrange for the incoming member of the Project Assurance Function to discuss the project and the Project Assurance Function role/relationship with the relevant Project Board member.

Project Assurance Function

3.6 Supporting Documents

1. Example of a Project Mandate.

2. Example of a Project Brief.

3. Example of a Handover Report.

4. Example of a Project Management Team Design Report.

5. Schematic diagram of the PRINCE organisation structure.

6. Summary of the responsibilities for each role in the PRINCE organisation structure.

7. Example of a Method of Approach Report.

8. Example of Terms of Reference for a member of the Project Management Team.

9. Example Agenda for a Project Start-Up Meeting.

10. Definition of the contents of a Product Description.

11. Example of a Business Case.

Project Assurance Function

EXAMPLE OF PROJECT MANDATE

Memo to: Mr. I Balance   **Finance Director**

From: Mr. Michael Cumbermack   **Managing Director**

Subject: **Strategic Planning Review**

Ivor,

At the Senior Management Retreat last month we discussed and agreed the strategic aims of the company for the forthcoming year. As you know this was documented in the policy paper XXXX.

At the strategy implementation committee we discussed the programme of work that will be needed to fulfill these aims and who should head up the three projects we decided to commission.

I have detailed below the project we would like you to undertake on behalf of the company.

Given
The Board of Ace Plumbing Supplies Ltd. have agreed that their business goal for this year will be:

> *To ensure continued Customer loyalty by providing a service level better than its competitors.*

To help meet this goal a Programme containing three major projects has been identified:

1)   To install a new switchboard.
2)   To upgrade the decoration of the Customer area and the trade counter.
3)   To develop a new sales and stock system.

The project we would like you to lead is number three.

Project Assurance Function

The reason for the projects (as you know only too well) is that the existing sales and stock system is now overstretched to the extent that it is inhibiting the growth of sales to both the trade and the public sectors.

The current system does not identify excess or out-of-date stocks and also has caused a number of errors when goods were sold when they were not in stock.

The sales manager has identified several new sales campaigns which require a list of current Customers - the present system cannot easily supply this.

What we need the project to do

To provide a new sales and stock system which will support the company's business goals.

The specific objectives are:

1) To ensure the sales section has easy access to details of the existing Customers to support new sales initiatives.
2) Ensure out of date or excess stock is easily identified.
3) To eliminate selling of 'stock' that does not exist.

Please come back to me if you have any questions.

Project Assurance Function

EXAMPLE OF PROJECT BRIEF

Project Background

The Board of Ace Plumbing Supplies Ltd. have agreed that their business goal for this year will be:

> *To ensure continued Customer loyalty by providing a service level better than its competitors.*

To help meet this goal a Programme containing three major projects has been identified:

1) To install a new switchboard.
2) To upgrade the decoration of the Customer area and the trade counter.
3) To develop a new sales and stock system.

This Project Brief is concerned with project number three.

The existing sales and stock system is now overstretched to the extent that it is inhibiting the growth of sales to both the trade and the public sectors.

The current system does not identify excess or out-of-date stocks and also has caused a number of errors when goods were sold when they were not in stock.

The sales manager has identified several new sales campaigns which require a list of current Customers - the present system cannot easily supply this.

Project Assurance Function

Project Aims and Objectives

The aim of the project is:

To provide a new sales and stock system which will support the company's business goals.

The specific objectives are:

1) To ensure the sales section has easy access to details of the existing User/*Customers* to support new sales initiatives.
2) Ensure out of date or excess stock is easily identified.
3) To reduce existing stock levels by 5%.
4) To eliminate selling of 'stock' that does not exist.

Scope and Constraints

Scope

The project is to concentrate its efforts on the sales and stock sections and its systems. Any links with other sections must be documented and defined.

The new system is to support the sales and stock sections, any other assistance it provides to other sections is not to be regarded as having any priority.

Assumptions that have been identified and agreed

The project is to be developed by an external development team.

The system must be easy to use.

The system must be able to cope with the expected growth of 30% this year and 15% for each successive year for the next five years.

The system must be able to supply word processing facilities for the management team.

The new system must not cost any more than £10,000 to install and have a running cost less than the existing manual systems and the project is to be completed during this financial year.

Project Assurance Function

Reporting

Ace Plumbing Supplies has given full responsibility for this project to a Project Board consisting of Mr. I Balance, Finance Manager (Executive), Mr. J Yorkshire, Sales Manager (Senior User/*Customer*) and Mr. J Kelly Senior Specialist Supplier, an external consultant engaged to advise Ace Plumbing Supplies.

The Project Board has full authority to proceed with this project within the limits of this document. If the Project Board expects to exceed this Brief then it must report to the full board of Ace Plumbing Supplies within seven days.

Project Assurance Function

EXAMPLE OF THE CONTENTS OF A HANDOVER REPORT

Role to be Handed Over:
Timing of the Hand Over:
Hand Over From:
Hand Over To:
Role receives Direction From/Reports To:
Role Description (usually an attachment):
Areas of Possible Role Description Change and Reasons:

Names, Locations, Phone/Fax Numbers of other Project Management Team Members:
Other Useful Contacts:

Project Team Members for whom the Role is Responsible:
Phone numbers and Locations of these Project Team Members:
Location of their Individual Work Plans:
Assessment of their Work (or reference to the location of such assessments):
Line Manager Responsible for each Team Member Allocated:
Arrangements for the Passage of Appraisal Information to Line Management:

Products for which the Role is Responsible:
Current Status of those Products:
Standards, Tools or Techniques being used for the Products:
Identifiers, Version Numbers and Location of the Products:

Current or Potential Problems Facing the Role:
Options and Recommendations:

Future Commitments for the Role:

Project Assurance Function

48

EXAMPLE OF A PROJECT MANAGEMENT TEAM DESIGN REPORT

To: **Ivor Balance**

From   J McCelland

Subject :   **Proposed Project Management Team Design for Sales and Stock Control Project.**

Introduction

The Sales and Stock Control Project is about to be initiated - however before we do so it is important that we consider and design a Project Management Team that will :

1. Effectively mange and control the project.
2. Ensure that the Specialist Suppliers receive appropriate guidance on what we require.
3. Relevant members of Ace Plumbing Supplies Staff are involved in the project.

The purpose of this paper is to describe the Project Management Team arrangements I propose to use to meet these requirements and the reasons behind the proposals. I would like to discuss these proposals with you and the board at their meeting at the end of the month.

Project Board

The PRINCE 2 methodology recommends that we set up a Project Board to represent the interest in the project, Business, User/*Customer*s, and the Supplier of the specialist skills needed to develop the project.

In looking at the scope of the project and the management team of Ace Plumbing and their skills and experience I recommend the following.

Project Assurance Function

Executive (Business Aspects)

Although inexperienced in projects which have a significant amount of computer technology and systems Mr. Ivor Balance (the Finance Director) does have both the required management experience and has in the past been involved with other types of project - particularly the new warehouse in Tottington.

Senior User/*Customer*

The choice of the Senior User/*Customer* was a little more difficult as this project affects both the sales and the stock control sections. The project has the greatest effect on the sales section and Mr. J Yorkshire (the current Sales Manager) did spend the first years of his career with Ace Plumbing in the stores section. Finally the only other contender Mr. H Stocks (Stock Control Manager) is due to retire next year so it seems sensible to appoint Mr. Yorkshire as Senior User/*Customer*.

Senior Specialist Supplier

Ace Plumbing will need to outsource a large part of the development of the new computer systems and also the management of the changes to the business processes that will occur as a consequence. Whilst we are quite capable of managing the changes to the business processes we have no one with in-depth experience of such a project to oversee the work of the Specialist Supplier we shall be using. It is vital that Ace Plumbing does have "Its Own Man" in this position so I propose that we appoint an independent consultant (not involved with the main contractor) to act as our Senior Specialist Supplier. The natural candidate for this is Mr. J Kelly from the MM&P consultancy who helped identify and define the need for this project last year.

I therefore propose to offer Mr. J Kelly a contract to be the Senior Specialist Supplier member of the Project Board.

Project Assurance Function

The Project Assurance Function is the responsibility of the members of the Project Board. In discussing this issue with each of them they felt that they would like to involve other members of the staff of Ace Plumbing Supplies as much as possible in the project so to this end they propose delegating the responsibly for project assurance to named individuals. These members of staff will report direct to the relevant member of the Project Board. The members of staff who have been selected are known for their independent nature and also their ability to handle change. After careful selection it has been decided to appoint the following members of staff to the Project Assurance Function as follows.

Project Assurance Function

50

Business Aspects
Mr. Ivor Solder has been with the Finance Department and latterly the Management Services Division. He has a good understanding of planning as he is studying this in his part time MBA course. His is keen to play an active role in the project and as such I propose him for this role.

User/*Customer* Aspects
As with the Senior User/*Customer* the choice of who to offer this role to was difficult. I am proposing Ms Louise Dargavel as she has an in-depth understanding of the sales side of the business from her activities as Progress Chaser. She also has first hand experience of the stock control system. However I have made it clear to Louise that she is not to make decisions herself rather to act as the co-ordinator of the User/*Customer* Liaison Forum which I am proposing later in this paper.

Specialist Supplier Aspects
Ace Plumbing Supplies has no member of staff who has the relevant technical knowledge to perform this role. As in the case of the Senior Specialist Supplier I propose to resort to the use of an external consultant. I have approached MM&P to supply such a person and having interviewed several possible candidates. I have chosen Mr. Trevor Whitlock. Trevor has performed this sort of role before for a similar project at United Widgets.

User/Customer Liaison Forum
To follow on from the wishes of the members of the Project Board to involve as many of the staff of Ace Plumbing in the decision making processes I propose to set up a User/*Customer* Liaison Forum which will be used to provide the Specialist Supplier with the information they require upon which to build the new computer and business systems. This Forum will be chaired by Mr. J Yorkshire and Mr. Stocks will act as deputy. The major active member of this Forum will be of course Ms Louise Dargavel.

Annexes

Job Descriptions and terms of reference for

1. Project Board members
2. Project Assurance Function
3. Chairman of the User/*Customer* Liaison Forum
4. ToR User/*Customer* Liaison Forum.

Project Assurance Function

51

PRINCE VERSION 2 ORGANISATION STRUCTURE

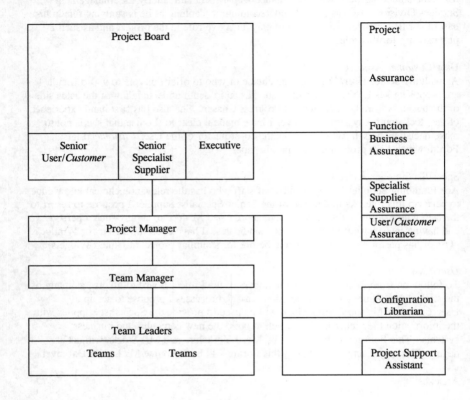

Project Assurance Function

SUMMARY OF ROLE RESPONSIBILITIES

Project Board

- To ensure that the project meets agreed standards of quality, time and cost.

- To ensure that the project remains viable against its Business Case.

- To provide overall guidance and control to the project.

Executive

- To represent the business interests of the organisation.

- To ensure the business integrity of the project.

- To ensure that the business Product of the project achieves the expected benefits.

- To ensure that the project is completed within the cost and timescale approved by the project approval authority.

- To chair the Project Board meetings.

Senior User/*Customer*

- To represent the interests of the User/*Customer* department(s) affected by the project.

- To monitor project progress against the requirements of the business Product's owner and User/*Customer* community.

- To commit the required User/*Customer* resources for approved Stage Plans.

- To have particular responsibility for the completeness and accuracy of the specification of requirements.

Project Assurance Function

Senior Specialist Supplier

- To ensure the Work Packages and Products developed by the Project Team adhere to the relevant standards and Codes of Practices.

- To represent the interests of the Specialist Supplier resources used in the project.

- To commit the Specialist Supplier resources required for approved Stage Plans.

Project Manager

- To ensure that the project as a whole produces the required technical, management and quality Products to the required standards needed for the project to achieve its expected business benefits.

- To plan the project to achieve its objectives within the given constraints.

- To monitor progress against plan.

- To advise the Project Board of any deviations from the plans and recommend any actions to be taken.

Team Manager

- To ensure production of a Stage's Work Packages or Products of appropriate quality within the constraints laid down by the Stage Plan.

- To assist the Project Manager in the preparation of the Stage Plan and agree on the viability of that plan.

Project Assurance Function

- To advise and assure the Project Board and other members of the organisation of the project's business and technical integrity. To assist other members of the organisation in the development and implementation of the project.

- To represent the interests of the Project Board and any other outside agencies, such as a separate Quality Assurance function.

Project Assurance Function

Business Aspects

- To provide business assurance for the project.

- To assist in the updating of the project's Business Case and monitor its continuing viability.

Specialist Supplier Aspects

- To advise on the standards, Codes of Practices and the tools and techniques that must be adhered to by the Project Team.

- To monitor the use of these standards, tools and techniques and bring any failings to the attention of the Team and Project Managers.

- To represent the interests of the Senior Specialist Supplier at a detailed level.

- To assist the Project and Team Managers with the preparation of the Project and Stage Plan.

User/*Customer* Aspects

- To represent the interests of the Senior User/*Customer* role at a detailed level.

- To provide information on the current system and its problems.

- To ensure details of new requirements are provided.

- To monitor Stage Products to ensure User/*Customer* requirements are met.

- To ensure that the final business Products meet the requirements.

Configuration Librarian

- To be guardian of all completed business Products and to release versions of the projects products.

- To administer the Project Issues procedures.

- To provide impact analysis data to evaluate potential changes.

Project Assurance Function

Project Support Function

To provide administrative assistance to the Project Manager

- To assist the Project Manager in :

  - Developing and updating Project and Stage Plans
  - Updating of the project's Business Case
  - Updating the Risk Analysis.
  - Administering the processing of Project Issues and O-SR and RFC
  - Administering the progress reporting process.
  - Administering and co-ordinating Quality Review activities.

Project Assurance Function

56

METHOD OF APPROACH REPORT

M E M O

To: J McCelland

From: Mr. J Kelly

Subject: Proposed Method of Approach for the Sales and Stock Control Project

Introduction

I was asked by the Project Manager, Jan McCelland, to prepare a paper to describe the Method of Approach I would recommend that is used to develop the above project. I have taken into account the experience of the members of staff in Ace Plumbing Supplies, the Project and Business Risk attached to the possible approaches, the proposed use of a package to meet the requirements and finally the timescales set for the project.

Conclusions

I wish to recommend to the Project Board that they adopt a two pass prototype approach to the development of the system using, for the analysis and design activities, the SSADM Version 4 method.

I have proposed this approach because it will not require the staff - particularly the proposed User/*Customer* Liaison forum to undertake too large a task in respect of reviewing complex documents.

In addition the use of the prototype method will enable the Specialist Supplier to demonstrate early on in the project that they have a firm understanding of what we require.

This approach is rapidly becoming the "Norm" for such projects as this i.e. Package Implementation with Minor Modifications. The choice of SSADM is based on the fact that the use of this almost standard approach will safeguard the organisation in the future as the diagrams can always be understood, it will also enable us to find a suitable consultant to be the member of staff responsible for the Project Assurance Function (Specialist Supplier aspects) without too much trouble. I have discussed this with the probable suppliers and they are all happy to proceed on this basis - so which ever of the three companies (IJM, Wavemans, Ulysses) is chosen I see no real problems.

Project Assurance Function

EXAMPLE OF TERMS OF REFERENCE FOR THE EXECUTIVE MEMBER OF THE PROJECT BOARD

M E M O

To:

From:

Subject: Executive Member of the Project Board - Project XX

Thank you for agreeing to be the Executive Member of the Project Board on the above project.

Attached to this memo are:

Annex 1   The agreed Job Description.
Annex 2   The Project Brief for the Project.
Annex 3   A section of the strategy programme plan for this project.
Annex 4   Progress Report format.

BACKGROUND TO THE PROJECT

This project is the "N"th in the programme agreed by the board on the 99/99/99 and is called X------------X.   The Project Manager responsible for the project has yet to be formally appointed, MX XXXXX.XXXXXX has been provisionally allocated to this role. No other members of the Project Management Team have been appointed as yet.

OBJECTIVES OF THE PROJECT

The project must produce the required products to the timescale and costs as defined in the Project Brief (which is attached to this memo).

In addition to these standard objectives the following additional ones have been identified:

Project Assurance Function

58

1.   You are to ensure that this project interfaces with project Y and the project X being launched on XXXXX.

2.   The User/*Customer* community must participate fully in the development of products to ensure that the implementation goes ahead on time as this project is the precursor to project W.

SCOPE AND CONSTRAINTS

As the Executive Member of the Project Board you have particular responsibility for reporting progress made with this project to the board.

The resources approved by the board for this project are defined in the attached Project Brief.

If during the development of the project you expect to exceed the time or resources allocated in the Project Brief then the board must be informed immediately.

Similarly if any of the resources allocated to the project are not made available for some reason, either in part or in whole, then the board must be informed immediately.

ASSUMPTIONS AND REPORTING

The assumptions that have been identified as being applicable to this project are:

e.g.   The products from project XX will be available to you.

The new operating system for the application will be available on XX.

You are to provide a monthly report on progress made to the board. The report will be in the format contained in annex 4.

Project Assurance Function

EXAMPLE OF TERMS OF REFERENCE FOR THE PROJECT MANAGER

MEMO

To:

From:

Subject: Project Manager - Project XX

Thank you for agreeing to be Project Manager on the above project.

Attached to this memo are:

Annex 1   The agreed Job Description
Annex 2   The Product Descriptions for the Products you are responsible for
Annex 3   The Project Mandate
Annex 4   Budget allocation and Progress Reporting Requirements

Background to the Project

This Project is the "N" th in the Strategic Programme called XXX and the Project has been named as XX. The provisional Project Board members allocated to the Start Up stage of the project are XX and XX.

Objectives of the Project

The Project must produce the required Products to the agreed timescale and costs. Product Descriptions for these products must be developed and agreed as part of the Project Initiation process.

You are to ensure the organisation's Quality Assurance Department is consulted about the Product Description for each of the Work Packages and Products that are the responsibility of the Specialist Supplier community.

Project Assurance Function

Scope and Constraints

As Project Manager you will be given full responsibility for the development of all the required Products

The resources given to you for this work are summarised in the attached spreadsheet and budget allocation paper.

During the development of the Products if you expect to exceed the time or resources allocated in the Mandate then the Project Board must be informed immediately. Similarly if any of the resources allocated to the Products in the Project and Stage Plan are not available in part or in whole then the Project Board must be informed immediately.

Assumptions and Reporting

The following assumptions have been identified as being applicable to this project:

e.g. The Products from project XX will be available to you.

.

The new operating system for the application will be available on XX.

You are to provide a Highlight Report on progress made to the Project Board at the end of each month. These reports will be in accordance with the format contained in the Organisations Standards (ref. XXXX). The details of when these reports are required are contained in the Progress Reporting Schedule contained in Annex 4.

Project Assurance Function

EXAMPLE OF TERMS OF REFERENCE FOR A TEAM MANAGER

M E M O

To:

From:

Subject: Team Manager - Project XX

Thank you for agreeing to be Team Manager on the above project.

Attached to this memo are:

Annex 1   The agreed Job Description
Annex 2   The Product Descriptions for the Products you are responsible for
Annex 3   The Stage Plan
Annex 4   Progress Reporting Schedule

Background to the Stage

This Stage is the "N" th in this project and is named as XX. The Project Manager responsible for the project is XX and the Project Board members are XX. The members of staff allocated to the Project Assurance Function allocated to this project are XX telephone numbers XX.

Objectives of the Stage

The Stage must produce the required Products to the agreed timescale and costs. Product Descriptions for these products are contained in the annex to this memo.

You are to ensure through the member of staff allocated to the Project Assurance Function in respect of the Specialist Supplier aspects that the organisation's Quality Assurance Department is consulted about the Product Description for each of the Work Packages and Products that are the responsibility of the Specialist Supplier community.

Project Assurance Function

Scope and Constraints

As Team Manager you will be given full responsibility for the development of Product numbers XX.

The resources given to you for this work are summarised in the attached Stage Plan Annex 3.

During the development of the Products if you expect to exceed the time or resources allocated in the Stage Plan then the Project Manager must be informed immediately. Similarly if any of the resources allocated to the Products in the Stage Plan are not available in part or in whole then the Project Manager must be informed immediately.

Assumptions and Reporting

The following assumptions have been identified as being applicable to this Stage of the project:

e.g. The Products from project XX will be available to you as shown in the Stage Plan.

The new operating system for the application will be available on XX.

You are to provide a Checkpoint Report on progress made to the Project Manager on completion of each of the Products. These reports will be in accordance with the format contained in the Project Initiation Document. The Project Manager will require assistance with the production of the Highlight Reports. The details of when these Reports are required are contained in the Progress Reporting Schedule contained in Annex 4.

Project Assurance Function

EXAMPLE OF TERMS OF REFERENCE FOR A MEMBER OF THE PROJECT ASSURANCE FUNCTION

M E M O

To:

From:

Subject: Project Assurance Function (User/*Customer*) - Project XXX

Thank you for agreeing to be the member of the Project Assurance Function responsible for the User/*Customer* aspects of the above project.

Attached to this memo are:

Annex 1   The agreed Job Description
Annex 2   The Product Initiation Document for the project (if available)

Background to your appointment

The XXX project is specifically designed to provide facilities for the sales and stock control departments:

You have been appointed as the (User/*Customer*) member of the Project Assurance Function (PAF).

The other members of the PAF are XXX (Business Aspects), XXX (Supplier Aspects). It is expected that you will work closely with the other members of the PAF. As the User/*Customer* member of the PAF you are to help XXX (the Senior User/*Customer* on the Project Board) to ensure that the User/*Customer*s interests are taken into account during the development of the project and that the eventual User/*Customer*s of the Products of this project are fully involved in their development.

Objectives

The objectives of the project are contained in the Project Initiation Document. Your specific role is defined in the agreed Job Description which is attached to this memo as Annex 1.

Project Assurance Function

64

In addition to these objectives the Senior User/*Customer* has requested that the following additional objectives are added to your Terms of Reference:

e.g. You are to ensure that the installation of the new system educates the User/*Customer* community as to the benefits of IT so that future projects can be easily assimilated into these User/*Customer* areas.

Scope and Constraints

As defined in your Job Description you are specifically responsible for the User/*Customer* area XXX. If other User/*Customer* areas outside of these defined in your Job Description are identified you are to bring them to the attention of the Senior User/*Customer* who will decide on what arrangements are to be made for representing those User/*Customer*s in this project.

The User/*Customer* department resources that are to be used in the development of the project are detailed in the Project Plan contained in the Project Initiation Document.

More detailed plans will be prepared prior to each Stage of the project commencing. You will be involved in identifying who from the User/*Customer* community should be involved, however you are not empowered to make any commitments on behalf of the User/*Customer* community except for any area that is within your existing line management responsibilities.

Assumptions and Reporting

The following assumptions can be regarded as being agreed:

- You can reallocate your existing duties to ensure you can devote the required time to your responsibilities in the project;

- the Senior User/*Customer* will be available for discussions about any areas of concern you have about the project.

Your reporting line for all project matters is to XXX the Senior User/*Customer* on the Project Board. All problems regarding User/*Customer* matters are ultimately the responsibility of the Senior User/*Customer* and therefore you should ensure that you regularly update the Senior User/*Customer* with an informal briefing to be given prior to the publication of the Highlight Reports and any Mid and End-Stage Assessments/Reports.

Project Assurance Function

EXAMPLE AGENDA FOR PROJECT START UP MEETING

1. Confirmation of the Project Brief/Project Mandate.

2. Confirmation of the Project Management Team structure, Job Definitions, roles and responsibilities.

3. Confirmation of the Method Of Approach Report.

4. Confirmation and approval of the draft plan for the Project Initiation Stage.

Project Assurance Function

DEFINITION OF THE CONTENTS OF A PRODUCT DESCRIPTION

Product Title:
Product Description

Purpose:
To describe the content, layout and quality specifications of a Product required to be built by the project. It also indicates the source(s) of data from which the Product is to be derived. The reasons for writing a Product Description are to:

- ensure by documenting it that the Product is sufficiently understood to enable its production to be planned, i.e. effort required, who needs to be involved, what dependencies does it have, how its completion will be checked;
- provide its creator with an accurate and complete description of what is required and to what quality measurements it will be submitted;
- provide the reviewers of the final Product with a series of measurements against which the Product can be judged in terms of its completeness and quality.

Composition:
Product Title
Product Reference
Purpose
Composition
Form/Format
Derivation
Quality Criteria
Method of checking its quality

(The composition will be absorbed within the Configuration Item Description Record in a Configuration Management Method.)

Form:
Identification of the standard form to be used, format of the document or method of presentation of the Product.

Project Assurance Function

Derivation:
Sources (prior Products, documents or individuals) from which the data for the Product are to be gathered.

Quality Criteria:
Measurable quality criteria for the Product. These may be standards to be used in its construction, references to checklists to be used to verify its accuracy, or questions to be asked about the finished Product.

Method:
The method(s) to be used to check the final Product. This may be a formal or informal Quality Review, a specific type of test or any other method which will be used to validate the Product.

Project Assurance Function

EXAMPLE OF A BUSINESS CASE

Project Aim

To provide the Senior Managers of Ace Plumbing Supplies with up to date information on current stocks and sales.

Project Objectives

- To ensure that sales are not made for items not in stock.
- To ensure that slow or non-moving stock is identified on a weekly basis.
- To enable the level of stock held to be reduced by 10%.
- To provide accurate and up to date information on Customers and purchases.

Project Scope

The scope of the project is the sales and stock section of Ace Plumbing Supplies.

Project Life

The project is a long term investment and as such the project life has been agreed as four years.

Options Examined

1 **Improvements to the existing system**
This option will involve improving the existing manual system by updating the records currently held by the sales section and by carrying out a full stock check every week to ensure the stock records are accurate.

2 **Installation of a partial computer system**
This option will involve installing a computer system to hold details of the stocks held by Ace Plumbing or details of the sales made to its Customers.

3 **Installation of an integrated sales and stocks computer system**
This option is to provide an integrated computer system that will hold details of all stocks and sales made by Ace Plumbing with an on-line interrogation facility.

Project Assurance Function

Risk and Sensitivity Analysis

The majority of the benefits from the project come from the computerisation of the stock control system. This area must be closely controlled. The sales information does not provide substantial benefits and if any problems occur with the project development then this aspect could be removed from the project.

The project is not critical for money however it is important that the benefits are realised. To this end we will extend the development life cycle into benefits realisation and keep the project in place until this product has been completed.

Recommendations

Proceed with Option 3 with a possible reversion to Option 2a if difficulties emerge with the sales section aspects of the project.

COST AND BENEFITS SUMMARY

	Year 0	Year 1	Year 2	Year 3	Year 4
Option 1					
Costs					
Consultants to review existing system	10000		10000		
Overtime to update records	3000		3000		
	13000		13000		
Benefits					
Reduction in sales errors	6000	6000	6000	6000	6000
Additional sales	2000	2000	2000	2000	2000
	8000	8000	8000	8000	8000

Project Assurance Function

70

Option 2
a) Stocks

Costs

	Year 1	Year 2	Year 3	Year 4	Year 5
Provision of Computer System	3000			3000	
Conversion of Records	2000				
	5000			3000	

Benefits

	Year 1	Year 2	Year 3	Year 4	Year 5
Reduction in stocks	2500	250	250	250	250
Reduction in Sales errors	8000	8000	8000	8000	8000
	10500	8250	8250	8250	8250

Option 2
b) Sales

Costs

	Year 1	Year 2	Year 3	Year 4	Year 5
Provision of Computer System	3000			3000	
Conversion of Records	2000				
	5000			3000	

Benefits

	Year 1	Year 2	Year 3	Year 4	Year 5
Additional Sales	4000	4000	4000	4000	4000
	9000	4000	4000	4000	4000

Project Assurance Function

71

Option 3

Costs

Provision of Computer System	5000			5000	
Conversion of records	5000				
	10000			5000	

Benefits

Reduction in Sales errors	8000	8000	8000	8000	8000
Reduction in stocks	2500	250	250	250	250
Additional Sales	2000	2000	2000	2000	2000
	12500	10250	10250	10250	10250

Project Assurance Function

COMPARISON

Option 1

Costs	13000			13000	
Benefits	8000	8000	8000	8000	8000
	(5000)	8000	8000	(5000)	8000
Discount Factor	1.0	.934	.877	.826	.781
Net Present Value(NPV)	(5000)	7472	7016	(4130)	6248
Cum NPV	(5000)	2472	9488	5358	11606

Option 2 a)

Costs	5000			3000	
Benefits	10500	8250	8250	8250	8250
	5500	8250	8250	8250	8250
Discount Factor	1.0	.934	.877	.826	.781
Net Present Value	5500	7706	7235	4336	6443
Cum NPV	5500	13206	20441	24777	31220

Option 2 b)

Costs	5000			3000	
Benefits	4000	4000	4000	4000	4000
	1000	4000	4000	1000	4000
Discount Factor	1.0	.934	.877	.826	.781
Net Present Value	1000	3736	3508	826	3124
Cum NPV	1000	4736	8244	9070	12194

Project Assurance Function

Option 3

Costs	10000			5000	
Benefits	12500	10250	10250	10250	10250
	2500	10250	10250	5250	10250
Discount Factor	1.0	.934	.877	.826	.781
Net Present Value	2500	9573	8989	4336	8005
Cum NPV	2500	12073	21062	25398	33403

Project Assurance Function

4. PROJECT INITIATION

4.1   Objectives of the Process

Every successful project must follow the basic concept of that "If you don't plan to control it from day one - then that's when it starts to go wrong".

To plan to succeed with a project means that the Project Manager and the organisation must ensure before the project starts in earnest that:

- the projects aims and objectives are documented and agreed;

- the Business Case for the project has been established and accepted (i.e. the baseline situation and the benefits that the project is to provide are defined and agreed);

- the organisation formally recognises the existence of the project;

- the organisation agrees to provide the required resources and support (manpower and money).

The Project Initiation process ensures that this happens through the development of a Project Initiation Document and agreement to it. The title Project Initiation Document is a slight misnomer in that the same document can be used in large projects to initiate a single phase. In addition the Project Initiation Document (PID) is also used throughout the project as the baseline against which any changes or modifications are assessed.

Project Assurance Function

It is not uncommon for an updated version of the PID to be prepared at the end of each Stage to reflect the increased understanding the project team then have of the project's objectives and costs. In such cases the original document remains as version one and subsequent versions exist as separate Products.

All such updating must be agreed by the Project Board who must ensure that the revised project remains consistent with the Project Mandate and Project Brief.

4.2   Description of the Process

The entire Project Management Team are involved in this process and it typically involves a number of iterations and versions of the Project Initiation Document.

The Project Manager takes the lead in the process by producing draft documents which are discussed with the members of the Project Management Team.

This can be a long process if the project is ill-defined in the Project Mandate or Project Brief or if the organisation does not have an effective project support infrastructure i.e. estimating and metrics data base and assistance with developing plans. If there is a lack of infrastructure it is that which causes the project initiation process to appear to take a long time NOT THE PROCESS ITSELF. Organisations which have an effective and comprehensive project support infrastructure can complete the initiation process in a few days.

Project Assurance Function

4.3   Possible Outputs

- IP1   Quality Plan
- IP2   Project Plan
- IP3   Defining/ refining the Business Case
- IP3A   Defining/ refining the Business and Project Risk
           Identification and Management Strategies
- IP4   Project Control Structure
- IP5   Project Filing System
- IP6   Project Initiation Document

Project Assurance Function

4.4   Checklist

A   Assist the Project Manager to prepare a Project Initiation Document which is within the agreed Project Brief for the project.

B   Examine the Project Level Product Flow Diagram and identify which of the Products are relevant to your area of responsibility. Examine their corresponding Product Descriptions and ensure you understand their contents

C   Attend the formal Quality Review of the Project Initiation Document. Particular attention must be paid to all Products are relevant to your area of responsibility in the Project Plans and Product Descriptions.

D   Be aware of the frequency, content and circulation dates of the Checkpoint and Highlight Reports.

E   Assist the Project Management Team to carry out a Risk Assessment of the project.

F   Discuss the Project Initiation Document informally with the relevant member of the Project Board. Particular attention should be paid to the proposed Quality Review and Product approval process.

G   Ensure the Project Board has approved and signed the Project Initiation Document.

Project Assurance Function

4.5   Guidance Notes

A   The Project Initiation Document contains the agreed basis of the project. The Project Initiation Document is amended by the Project Board on advice from the project Manager/Project Assurance Function. The amendment process continues until the Project Initiation Document is outside the Project Brief for the Project. When this occurs the Project Board will discuss the project with the PCA or Programme Board to re-establish the Project Brief.

When reviewing or proposing amendments to the Project Initiation Document the members of staff appointed to a Project Assurance Function role should pay particular attention to:

- the project scope/boundaries;
- the assumptions/constraints affecting the project;
- the Business Case for the project (if any);
- the resources and priorities allocated to this project.

If the Project Initiation Document appears to be at variance to the Project Brief then the members of staff allocated to the Project Assurance role must discuss this with the relevant member of the Project Board so that they can refer it to the PCA or Programme Board to consider changes to the Project Brief.

The Project Initiation Document should be developed in Stages and agreed with the Project Board in a series of informal meetings. A "big bang" approach usually results in a very long Project Initiation Meeting and considerable rework.

B   The Project Level Product Flow Diagram is designed to show only the most important or significant Products or Work Packages.

Project Assurance Function

They can be regarded as "suitcase Products" i.e. they contain many sub Products.

The name selected for the Work Package or Project Level Product normally coincides with the last of its sub Products (the last in the chain!).

The members of the Project Assurance Function should also inspect each of the Project Level Product Descriptions (which are within their area of responsibility) and their associated Quality Criteria. The members of the staff allocated to the Project Assurance Function should look for any links between the Products in this project and any other project. If the members of the Project Assurance Function have any doubts about potential links these should be discussed with the Project and Team Manager. When such links between Products are identified it is vital that the Product Descriptions and Quality Criteria for those Products do correspond. In addition to identifying such links the Project Assurance Function may also provide input to the definition and contents of the Product Descriptions and the Quality Criteria.

This procedure for defining which Products or Work Packages are to be shown in the Product Flow Diagram is different in each organisation. Generally, the Project Manager assumes responsibility for the development of the first draft of the Product Flow Diagram. However, it is not unusual for the members of the Project Assurance Function to be involved in defining the Product Descriptions and deciding the sequence of the products in the Product Flow Diagram.

The process of how the Product Descriptions and the Product Flow Diagram will be developed will have been described on the

PRINCE training course you attended. The following list may refresh your memory:

- examine any previous projects or standard life cycles to identify potential component Products for this project;
- reflect the needs of this specific project or development environment in the list of Products;
- refine and update the Product Descriptions to ensure that all the required Products have been identified;
- amend the Product Descriptions to include any modifications required (those that were identified when they were used on previous projects);
- discuss and agree these modifications as appropriate with the User/*Customer* and Specialist Supplier community.

C The Project Manager has responsibility for the production of the Project Initiation Document. The first draft of the Project Initiation Document must be formally Quality Reviewed prior to its submission to the Project Board for their approval.

The members of the Project Assurance Function should attend this review. They will also need to ensure that appropriate Reviewers are identified for each of the sections of the Project Initiation Document and that this "technical" review process is completed. It is sometimes difficult to identify suitable people for this task particularly in small organisations and as a consequence the members of the Project Assurance Function may have to perform all the required tasks.

D PRINCE has a comprehensive set of progress or management reports.

Project Assurance Function

Checkpoint and Highlight Reports are important regular reports to the Project Manager and Project Board.

It is important that the members of the Project Assurance Function ensure that the reports:

- provide the required information for their intended audience;
- are produced and distributed at the frequency required by the Project Board;
- distributed to the people who need them.

To ensure that these reports are effective the members of the Project Assurance Function should confirm, before the project starts, with the relevant members of the Project Board and the organisation, who should have them and their format and content.

The cost of producing these management reports can be high so it is advisable to generate as much as possible automatically from any planning software that may be used on the project. This is achieved by collecting information on the resources used and comparing this to the plan contained on the planning software.

Some of the better software can provide complete Checkpoint and Highlight reports. None of the software currently available can fully analyse the reasons for any late or non delivery. This analysis must be done by the Project Manager and the members of the Project Assurance Function and any conclusions reached included in the report.

Once the discussion on the format, contents, and frequency of these reports is complete, it is usual for the Project Support Assistant to produce a list of the publication dates and who is responsible for the development and circulation of the reports. This information should be included in the Project Initiation Document.

E   As part of deciding whether the project is a good investment of company resources, a Risk Assessment is prepared and included in the Project Initiation Document. The main participants in this are the Project Manager and the member/s of the Project Assurance Function responsible for the business aspects of the project The member/s of the Project Assurance Function responsible for User/*Customer* aspects should also contribute information and opinions on the User/*Customer* viewpoint of the risks facing the project.

F   The theme of PRINCE formal meetings is "no surprises". This means that before the formal presentation of the Project Initiation Document to the Project Board, one of your tasks is to meet the relevant member of the Project Board and informally discuss all the aspects of the document for which you are both responsible and identify any questions you have about its contents. This is a major part of your assurance function. In order to carry it out successfully you will have to get a thorough understanding of the Project Initiation Document and its contents.

G   The Project Manager should present the Project Initiation Document to the Project Board for its approval. The approval process is best accomplished in Stages by informal discussions of the draft document prior to its formal approval. It should not be presented without this prior discussion unless it is a very small project.

Project Assurance Function

Failure to adopt this phased approach may mean that the Project Initiation Meeting will take a long time, result in considerable changes to the document, and as a consequence delay the start of the project.

The following list describes the typical steps in these informal discussions:

- agree with each of the members of the Project Management Team their role and Job Descriptions and check the Project Brief is still valid;
- develop and agree a list of Products or Work Packages to be produced and a project development strategy with the Project Board members;
- agree the Product Flow Diagram and Project Plans with the Project Board members;
- complete the Project Initiation Document and hold the Project Initiation Meeting. Ensure the Project Board pays particular attention to the Risk Assessment section of the Project Initiation Document.

The Project Assurance Function should be involved in this process and assist the Project Manager with the development of the Project Initiation Document. Use of the approach described above will ensure that the Project Board meeting to agree the Project Initiation Document is both short and effective.

Project Assurance Function

4.6 Supporting Documents

1. Example of a Project Initiation Document.

2. Example of Checkpoint, Highlight Reports.

3. Example of Project Initiation Meeting Agenda.

4. Example of a checklist for deciding the level of Quality Review.

5. Schematic diagram of the component parts of PRINCE plans.

EXAMPLE OF PROJECT INITIATION DOCUMENT

INTRODUCTION

The purpose of this Project Initiation Document is to provide a statement of the environment and Products required from the project to support the business goals of the organisation.

The Project Initiation Document has been prepared to ensure that the Project Board and the Project Management Team have an agreed understanding of the system to be developed. It will be used by the Project Board to define the initial objectives of the project to develop the stock and sales administration system. It contains the baseline plan which will be used to monitor and control the development of the new system.

CONFIRMED PROJECT BRIEF

Project Background

The Board of Ace Plumbing Supplies Ltd. have agreed that their business goal for this year will be:

> *To ensure continued Customer loyalty by providing a service level better than its competitors.*

To help meet this goal three major projects have been identified:

1   To install a new switchboard.
2   To upgrade the decoration of the Customer area and the trade counter.
3   To develop a new sales and stock system.

This Project Brief is concerned with project number three.

The existing sales and stock system is now overstretched to the extent that it is inhibiting the growth of sales to both the trade and the public sectors.

The current system does not identify excess or out of date stocks and also has caused a number of errors when goods were sold when they were not in stock.

Project Assurance Function

The sales manager has identified several new sales campaigns which require a list of current Customers - the present system cannot easily supply this.

Project Aims and Objectives

The aim of the project is:

To provide a new sales and stock system which will support the company's business goals.

The specific objectives are:

1   To ensure the sales section has easy access to details of the existing Customers to support new sales initiatives.
2   Ensure out of date or excess stock is easily identified.
3   To reduce existing stock levels by 5%.
4   To eliminate selling of stock that does not exist.

Scope and Constraints

Scope

The project is to concentrate its efforts on the sales and stock sections and its systems. Any links with other sections must be documented and defined.

The new system is to support the sales and stock sections, any other assistance it provides to other sections is not to be regarded as having any priority.

Assumptions that have been identified and agreed

The project is to be developed by an external development team.

The system must be easy to use.

The system must be able to cope with the expected growth of 30% this year and 15% for each successive year for the next five years.

The system must be able to supply word processing facilities for the management team.

The new system must not cost any more than £10,000 to install and have a running cost less than the existing manual systems.

The project is to be completed during this financial year.

Project Assurance Function

Reporting

Ace Plumbing Supplies has given full responsibility for this project to a Project Board consisting of Mr. I Balance, Finance Manager (Executive), Mr. J Yorkshire, Sales Manager (Senior User/*Customer*) and Mr. J Kelly (Senior Specialist Supplier) an external consultant engaged to advise Ace Plumbing Supplies.

The Project Board has full authority to proceed with this project within the limits of this document. If the Project Board expects to exceed this Brief then it must report to the full board of Ace Plumbing Supplies within five days of this becoming apparent.

BUSINESS CASE

Project Scope

The scope of the project is the sales and stock section of Ace Plumbing Supplies.

Project Life

The project is a long term investment and as such the project life has been agreed as four years.

Options Examined

1   Improvements to the existing system

   This option will involve improving the existing manual system by updating the records currently held by the sales section and by carrying out a full stock check every week to ensure the stock records are accurate.

2   Installation of a partial computer system

   This option will involve installing a computer system to hold details of the stocks held by Ace Plumbing or details of the sales made to its Customers.

3   Installation of an integrated sales and stocks computer system

   This option is to provide an integrated computer system that will hold details of all stocks and sales made by Ace Plumbing with an on-line interrogation facility.

Project Assurance Function

Risk and Sensitivity Analysis

The majority of the benefits from the project come from the computerisation of the stock control system. This area must be closely controlled. The sales information does not provide substantial benefits and if any problems occur with the project development then this aspect could be removed from the project.

The project is not critical for money. However it is important that the benefits are realised. To this end we will extend the development life cycle into benefits realisation and keep the project in place until this Product has been completed.

Recommendations

Proceed with Option 3.

Project Assurance Function

COSTS AND BENEFITS SUMMARY

Option 3	Year 0	Year 1	Year 2	Year 3	Year 4
Costs					
Provision of Computer System	5000			5000	
Conversion of records	5000				
	10000			5000	
Benefits					
Reduction in Sales errors	8000	8000	8000	8000	8000
Reduction in stocks	2500	250	250	250	250
Additional Sales	2000	2000	2000	2000	2000
	12500	10250	10250	10250	10250
Option 3					
Costs	10000			5000	
Benefits	12500	10250	10250	10250	10250
	2500	10250	10250	5250	10250
Discount Factor	1.0	.934	.877	.826	.781
Net Present Value	2500	9573	8989	4336	8005
Cum NPV	2500	12073	21062	25398	33403

Project Assurance Function

DEFINITION OF ORGANISATION AND RESPONSIBILITIES

Project Board

- Mr. I Balance,   Finance Manager   Executive
- Mr. J Yorkshire,   Sales Manager   Senior User/*Customer*
- Mr. J Kelly,   External consultant   Senior Specialist Supplier

Project Manager

Jan McClelland

Project Assurance Function

- Ivor Solder   Business Aspects
- Louise Dargavel   User/*Customer* Aspects
- Trevor Whitlock   Specialist Supplier Aspects

Copies of roles and job descriptions are attached as Annex x.

PROJECT PLAN

This section contains a summary of the information contained in the Project Plan and the accompanying Product Breakdown Structures, Product Flow Diagrams and Product Descriptions. These are contained in Annex x.

Stage 1

Work Package One: Products 1 and 2.

To be completed by 16th March

Budget £1,000

Project Assurance Function

91

Work Package Two: Products 3, 4, 5, 7 and 8.

To be completed by 24th May

Budget £1,500

Stage 3

Work Package Three and Four: Products 6 and 9 to 16.

To be completed by 30th July

Budget £6,000

Stage 4

Work Package Five and Six: Products 17,18, 19 and 20.

To be completed by 16th October

Budget £1,500

Total Cost £10,000

Project Tolerance +10 days, +£1,000

QUALITY PLAN

Product Descriptions: will be prepared for all the Products to be developed. These will be agreed with the members of the Project Assurance Function at the creation of the plan in which the Products appear.

Quality Reviews: each Product will be subjected to either a formal or an informal Quality Review. The level of review and the review teams will be agreed by the Project Management Team when creating the plan in which the Products are created.

Documentation: all reviews will be fully documented. Examples of the documents to be used are attached as Annex x.

Project Assurance Function

Controls and Reporting Arrangements: Checkpoint Reports will be produced at the completion of every Product. Highlight Reports every four weeks and circulated to the Project Board. Mid-Stage Assessments will be held if (in the opinion of the Project Manager) an Exception Report is raised that requires a meeting of the Project Board. All other arrangements will be as defined in the PRINCE reporting standards. Example proformas of all the reports are attached as Annex x.

PROJECT PREREQUISITES

All members of Ace Plumbing Supplies who will have a Project Management Team role must receive appropriate PRINCE training.

EXTERNAL DEPENDENCIES

The development is dependent on the issue of a new version of the operating system by Mickey Mousesoft.

PLAN ASSUMPTIONS

Suitable space will be found at Ace Plumbing Supplies to locate the computer.

The current records can be converted to the new system.

Ace Plumbing Staff will be made available in accordance with the agreed Stage Plans.

PROJECT RISK ASSESSMENT

A full Risk Assessment has been carried out. The results are held in Annex x. The result of the assessment is that the project risk is low.

CONFIGURATION MANAGEMENT PLAN

Note - in this project the role of Configuration Librarian will be shared by the Project Support Assistant and Specialist Supplier team members.

Each Product will be uniquely identified by a reference number allocated by the Project Support Assistant. It will contain the Product number, version number and type.

Configuration Control will be exercised by Project Support Assistant, who will store and issue Product copies as required.

Project Assurance Function

93

All Project Issue will be logged and controlled by the Project Manager. The procedures for evaluation and processing of the Project Issue Reports will be in accordance with the PRINCE manual.

ANNEXES

Job Descriptions
  Project Board
  Project Manager
  Team Manager
  Project Assurance Function

Project Plans
  Product Flow Diagram
  Work Package and Product Breakdown Structure
  Project Plan
  Supporting Narrative

Quality Review Proformas
  QR Invitation
  QR Error List
  QR Result Notification
  QR Action List

Reporting Proformas
  Checkpoint Report
  Highlight Report
  ESM Agenda
  Risk Assessment Checklist

Project Assurance Function

EXAMPLE CHECKPOINT REPORT

CHECKPOINT REPORT					
From:		**To:**		**For products:**	
Product ID	**Product Name**	**Due to Start**	**Actual Start**	**Due to Cmplte**	**Actual Cmpltn**

Project Assurance Function

95

EXAMPLE HIGHLIGHT REPORT

HIGHLIGHT REPORT				
From:	**To:**		**For period:**	
ID No / **Product Name**	**Due to complete**	**Actual completion**	**Comments**	

Variances Analysis		**Max**	**Min**	**Av**	**Comments**
	% Resources				
Product Production	**% Cost**				
	% Delay				
Problems/Opportunities Encountered					
Impact on Rest of Stage/Product					

Project Assurance Function

EXAMPLE AGENDA FOR A PROJECT INITIATION MEETING

1. Confirmation of Project Initiation Document.

2. Confirmation of the First Stage Plan.

Project Assurance Function

97

EXAMPLE OF A CHECKLIST FOR DECIDING LEVEL OF QUALITY REVIEW REQUIRED

FACTOR	CONSIDER		PROBABLE	
	Formal	Informal	Formal	Informal
New product to the organisation			xx	
Final product (deliverable)			xx	
Interim product (non-deliverable)	xx			xx
Small component of another product	xx			xx
Links with Work Packages and or Products outside project	xx		xx	
"Politically" sensitive			xx	
Standards newly defined	xx		xx	
Product well known (common)	xx			xx
Developers new to product			xx	
End of Stage product			xx	
Product will be revised later in project	xx			xx
Problems with this product previously			xx	
Key product in development			xx	
New development technique used			xx	
Quality Reviewers very experienced		xx		
Quality Reviewers very inexperienced			xx	

Project Assurance Function

98

PRINCE PLAN STRUCTURE

Project Plan

Product Breakdown Structure

Product Flow Diagram

Work Package and Product Descriptions

Gantt or Bar Chart

Resource Spreadsheet

Plan Description

Stage Plan

Product Breakdown Structure

Product Flow Diagram

Work package and Product Descriptions

Gantt or Bar Chart

Resource Spreadsheet

Plan Description

Team Plan

List of tasks/Product Descriptions

or

Gantt or Bar Chart

Resource Spreadsheet

Project Assurance Function

99

5   CONTROLLING A STAGE

5.1   Objectives of the Process

This process is the one that manages the project on a day to day basis once the Project Board have given approval for the work to proceed. As with all the elements of the PRINCE method it seeks to manage this work in a controlled environment or way.   The purpose of this controlled environment is not to stifle creativity in the Project Manager or the Project Management Team rather to give them some "stepping stones" to use on their difficult task of creating a unique outcome through a unique set of Products.

The objectives of the process are to ensure that:

- the required Products are delivered;

- the Products are developed to the agreed quality standards;

- the allocated resources (money, materials, manpower, timescales) are not exceeded;

- the Project Management Team are given timely and accurate direction;

- the Project and Stage Plans are regularly updated and the progress made monitored;

- any major deviation/s from the plans in respect of Products or resource usage are corrected as appropriate;

Project Assurance Function

100

- all interested parties are informed about project progress;

- the project is stopped or redirected if it is apparent that it will not meet the business need or the business need itself has changed.

5.2   Description of the Process

This process starts after the approval of each Stage Plan by the Project Board and continues until the end of that Stage. The order of the constituent processes described in this section attempt to follow the typical sequence that will be found in a project, this of course means that the sequence will need to be amended to reflect the needs of each specific project and the events that occur in it.

The processes are designed to work with those in process MP - managing a Product Delivery and DP Directing the Project. In reality the Project Manager may chose to hybrid these three PRINCE processes together as the Controlling a Stage Process is predominately about ensuring the agreed Products are delivered to the defined quality standard and within the agreed resource allocation.

The process starts with the definition and authorisation of the Work Package   that the Stage is to deliver. This then moves to the MP Process which controls the delivery of that package whilst this process continues with the regular assessment of progress made and recording the consumption of resources expended CS2, 5 and 6. These two processes also link with the DP process which feed the information and assurance to the Project Board. The remainder of the process in this process are directed at the management and control of Project Issues.

Project Assurance Function

101

As Project Issues may be submitted at any time during a Stage and there may be a number of them submitted at various times process number CS3,4,7,8 may need to be repeated a number of times and indeed a number of each individual ones may be underway at one time.

The control of Project Issues is one of the most important duties of the Project Manager as they can lead to the scope and direction of the project moving away from that agreed by the Project Board and the organisation.

5.3   Outputs to be Produced by this Process

- CS1   Work Package Authorisation and definition

- CS2   Progress Assessment Reports

- CS3   Project Issue Receipt Report

- CS4   Project Issue Evaluation Report

- CS5   Stage Status Assessment Report

- CS6   Highlight Reports

- CS7   Corrective Action Report

- CS8   Project Board Assessment of Project Issue Report

- CS9   Receipt of Completed Work Package Report

Project Assurance Function

5.4   Checklist

A   Ensure each User/*Customer*, Specialist Supplier oriented Product is Quality Reviewed to the agreed PRINCE standard.

B   Ensure that any comments on the Quality Review process made by the reviewers are followed up.

C   Attend any project progress meetings that the Project Manager arranges.

D   Ensure that the Project and Team Managers are being provided with (and use) the appropriate members of the User/*Customer* and Specialist Supplier community in developing the Work Packages and Products.

E   Review the Checkpoint and Highlight Reports produced by the Team Manager and Project Manager.

F   Review any reports on the progress of the project to the Project Board and the rest of the organisation, that are prepared by the Team and Project Managers.

G   Provide day to day support to all members of the Project Management Team involved in this Stage.

H   Assist the Project/Team Manager to produce any Exception Plans that are required.

I   Assist the Project/Team Manager to process Project Issues and the resulting Off Specification Reports and Requests For Change.

Project Assurance Function

103

5.5   Guidance Notes

A   It may be desirable for one of the members of the Project Assurance Function to be involved with all the formal Quality Reviews as a reviewer.   In very large projects this practice may prove to be physically impossible, or it may not be economic.

Therefore, it is essential for the members of the Project Assurance Function to decide which of the Quality Review meetings to attend. The main factors to consider are:

- have you confidence in the ability of the Reviewers?
- have the User/*Customer* and Specialist Supplier oriented Reviewers got the confidence of others?
- have you confidence in the Chairman?
- is the Product vital to the project?
- have there been problems with the Product or this type of Product before?

You must check on behalf of the Project Board that the reviews at which you were not present were carried out to the correct standard.   Typically answering the following questions will give you sufficient information to judge the quality of the review:

- how long were the Reviewers given to look at the Product/s prior to the meeting?
- how many and what type of errors were identified prior to the meeting?
- what was the outcome of the review?
- how long did the review meeting last?

Project Assurance Function

104

It is also useful to talk to the Reviewers to find out if they were happy with the conduct of the review and its outcome. (For details of the Quality Review procedures see the PRINCE Manual.)

If any of these give course for concern you should tell the Project Manager and ask for a more detailed investigation.

B   The Quality Review documents used on most projects contain space for the Reviewers and the Chairman to make additional comments about the review - these comments are usually concerned with either the Quality Criteria or the Product Description.

You should read each Quality Review Report, and where any comments were made, discuss them with the appropriate member of the Project Assurance Function and the Reviewers (or whoever made the comments) to determine what were the problems and what has to be done to remedy the situation.

You must satisfy yourself that any follow-up action needed was carried out and approved. This follow-up is important if the organisation is to learn from its problems and to stop them happening again in future projects.

C   The PRINCE method does not provide all the progress reporting required by an organisation. It is common for the Project/Team Manager to hold additional meetings to review the project's progress. These meetings will consider the progress made (as shown by the Stage File and associated reporting systems) and should concentrate on any lessons learnt and the impact on the project of any variations from the plan that have been identified.

Project Assurance Function

These meetings are also a valuable forum for the Project Manager to inform the members of Project Assurance Function of the results of any discussions with the Project Board, or information on events from outside the project which may affect its development.

[Note: The members of the Project Assurance Function should include such information in the briefings provided to their respective member of the Project Board.]

D The members of the Project Assurance Function should ensure that the Project and Team Managers are notified of any members of the organisation they believe should be involved in the development of the Work Packages or Products in this Stage. In addition they should also monitor whether these members of staff were involved in the development and whether they believe that their input has been acted upon. If this has not been the case then the member of the Project Assurance Function must discuss this with the Project and Team Manager and identify the reasons or cause of this dissatisfaction.

If they are concerned that this has compromised the integrity of the Product or Work Package they must formally report and discuss this with the relevant member of the Project Board as soon as possible.

E The members of the Project Assurance Function should attend, when possible, the Checkpoint meetings and, particularly if the Stage Plan shows that Products or Work Package important to the area for which they are responsible are in production.

At the beginning of a project it should have been defined when the Checkpoint and Highlight Reports are to be created, and the members of the Project Assurance Function should review these and if appropriate comment on their content.

Each progress report should be examined to identify where the project varies significantly from the plan.

At the beginning of a Stage the members of the Project Assurance Function must by informed by the Project and Team Manager what is a significant variance, e.g. a time variance of x days, otherwise this analysis may not prove to be economic or useful.

The analysis of any significant variance should address the following questions:

- did development of the Product start on time?
- did the development finish on time?
- are there notes on the Checkpoint and Highlight Reports which explain why they were delayed?
- were the appropriate standards used?
- were alternative resources or methods used to develop the Product?
- were any quality tasks dropped or cut short to avoid budget or schedule overruns?

As a result of this analysis you may need to carry out a follow-up or more detailed investigation to identify any required remedial action.

The members of the Project Assurance Function should ensure that the Highlight Reports are produced on time, to the agreed standard, and circulated to the relevant members of the Project Board.

Project Assurance Function

F   When asked to provide ad-hoc or special reports to others in the organisation who are not directly involved in the project you must ensure that you have the permission of the Project Manager or the Project Board to provide the information. It is recommended that one of the Products produced early in the project is the Communication Strategy. This document will define who can and will, talk to who about what about the project.

G   Other User/*Customer*s involved occasionally in the project may be untrained in the PRINCE methods. It is recommended that the members of the Project Assurance Function identify any training which is commensurate with their involvement.   One common requirement is support with the Quality Review procedure. This procedure will be a new experience for most of them and they will need support in order to understand the Quality Review procedures and techniques and why these Reviews are required.

To be effective in this role you must make yourself aware of the PRINCE training courses used by the organisation.

H   During a Stage there may be a need to prepare an Exception Report. An Exception Report is needed when:

- Products are late or cannot be produced;
- there is a need to change a Product that has already been produced (RFC or OSR);
- a Product expected from another project has not arrived.
- any other incident has occurred which potentially affects the project.

Project Assurance Function

When these situations occur the members of the Project Assurance Function should bring it to the Project and Team Managers' attention to:

- assess the impact of the problem;
- identify potential solutions/options;
- determine the costs/benefits of the proposed solutions/options;
- prepare a report to the Project Board on the situation that caused the problem and to discuss the contents of a possible recovery or Exception Plan.

The exact form that this assistance will take will be determined by the situation that has arisen and the way that PRINCE is used in your organisation.

If the matter that has arisen to cause the Exception Report has a significant effect on the project then a Mid Stage Assessment meeting will be held by the Project Board to discuss the situation.

At this meeting the Project Board may request the Project Manager to prepare an Exception Plan which describes how the problem should be tackled.

It is not uncommon for the Project Manager to pre-empt the Project Board's request to prepare an Exception Plan by preparing it prior to the Mid Stage Assessment Meeting and for it to be discussed then rather than at a second meeting.

I   The procedure for processing a Project Issue will involve the Project Manager, Team Manager and Project Assurance Function.

Project Assurance Function

109

The typical procedure for processing a Project Issue will have been described on the PRINCE training course that you attended. This procedure may be tuned to reflect your particular project and the way that PRINCE has been implemented in your organisation.

The key steps in the process in which the members of the Project Assurance Function are involved are:

- ensuring that all User/*Customer* and Specialist Supplier concerns potentially affected by the Project Issue are identified;

- the initial assessment of the importance of the Project Issue to the business is carried out quickly and effectively;

- the detailed analysis of the impact of the Project Issue is conducted by the Project Assurance Function and the Project and Team Manager promptly and effectively. (The development of an Exception Report and Plan is described in sub section H.).

- the decision on the conversion of the Project Issue to either a Request For Change or an Off Spec Report and the identification of who should approve the proposed action

- to assist the Project Manager in organising and implementing any User/*Customer* or Specialist Supplier action in modifications agreed by the Project Board (or Project Manager).

Project Assurance Function

110

5.6   Supporting Documents

1. Example of a Project Issue Evaluation Checklist.

2. Example Agenda for an unplanned Mid-Stage Assessment Meeting.

3. Example of a Mid-Stage Assessment Report and memo.

4. Example of a Summary of an Exception report and Exception Plan.

5. Example of a Completed Checkpoint Report.

6. Example of a Completed Highlight Report.

7. Example of a Metrics Collection Form.

Project Issue Evaluation Checklist

1. Have all fields on the PI been correctly filled in?
2. Has PI been logged?
3. Has a copy been returned to the originator?
4. Has a master copy been filed in the appropriate section of the Quality File?
5. Identify the cause of the PI.
   - Does it reflect a misunderstanding on the part of the originator? If so, someone should be delegated to write an explanation of the misunderstanding to the originator on a copy of the PI, which can then be closed.
   - Does the PI concern a product or topic outside the scope of this project? If so, the PI and PI Log should be updated to show that it has been passed to the correct authority and the PI closed.
   - Is it proposing a change to a baselined product? If so, a recommendation should be made to the Project Manager to convert the PI to a Request For Change (RFC).
   - Does it suggest that a baselined product does not meet its specification? If so, has sufficient supporting evidence been supplied? If it is relevant, could the problem be recreated from the provided evidence? A recommendation should be made to raise an Off-Specification Report (O-SR).
   - Does it record some inability on the part of the developer to meet some part of the agreed specification or design? If so, the conversion of the PI to an O-SR should be recommended.
   - Does it record a real or forecast inability to deliver the required Work Packages and or Products within the Tolerance constraints of the plans? If so, the conversion of the PI to an O-SR should be recommended.
6. Have all outstanding PIs been examined? If not, what is the status of those not reviewed? Are there good reasons why any PIs are not being reviewed?
7. After each PI meeting the reviewed PIs should be sent to the Project Manager with written recommendations on the action to be taken.
8. On return of the PIs with the Project Manager's decision, the filed master should be updated and a copy sent to the originator.

Project Assurance Function

Off-Specification Reports

9.   O-SRs should be assessed by the member of the Project Assurance Function responsible for Specialist Supplier Aspects for the amount of effort required to resolve them. This normally includes the Configuration Librarian, who will provide information on other affected Work Packages and or Products or projects. The assessment should include giving a priority to the O-SR (high, medium, low or cosmetic).

10. If the investigation reveals that it was incorrect to raise an O-SR, this should be documented on the O-SR and returned to the Project Manager for a new decision. It is in order for it to be converted to an RFC or the original PI to be re-opened then closed with a suitable reply to the originator.

11. The final part of the assessment is a classification. This is done by the Project Manager.
     -   Class 1 changes affect Work Packages and or Products which have already been approved and accepted as finished by the Project Board.
     -   Class 2 changes could not be carried out within the Tolerances set for the current Stage or for the project.
     -   Class 3 changes are those which could be done within the Tolerances of the Stage and the project.

12. The evaluated O-SRs are now returned to the Project Manager for decision on the action to be taken. Class 1 and 2 changes must cause an unplanned Mid Stage Assessment for the Project Board to consider what they want to do. They should be accompanied by an Exception Report/Plan showing the extra work which would be required during the current Stage towards implementing the changes. It may be that later Stages will also include some of the work, but that will appear in those Stage Plans.

13. It is sensible for the Project Manager to discuss the cases informally with the Project Board before preparing the Exception Report/Plan, so that it reflects what they are likely and willing to approve.

14. A Project Manager should plan to rectify Class 3 O-SRs within the plan. Again, not all of the corrective work may be in this Stage. Corrective work which will be done in later Stages will appear in the activities for those Stages.

Requests For Change

15. The member of the Project Assurance Function responsible for User/*Customer* Aspects should ensure that all RFCs are evaluated in terms of their benefit to the User/*Customer*. The assessment should include giving a priority to the RFC (high, medium, low or cosmetic).

Project Assurance Function

113

16. It may be that the RFC has been raised by one of the Specialist Suppliers staff, suggesting a better way of meeting requirements. These should still be assessed by the User/*Customer* community.

17. RFCs should be assessed by the member of the Project Assurance Function responsible for Specialist Supplier Aspects for the amount of effort required to resolve them. This normally includes the Configuration Librarian, who will provide information on other affected Work Packages and or Products or projects.

18. If the investigation reveals that it was incorrect to raise an RFC, this should be documented on the RFC and returned to the Project Manager for a new decision. It is in order for it to be converted to an O-SR or the original PI to be re-opened then closed with a suitable reply to the originator.

19. The final part of the assessment is a classification. This is done by the Project Manager
    - Class 1 changes affect Work Packages and or Products which have already been approved and accepted as finished by the Project Board.
    - Class 2 changes could not be carried out within the Tolerances set for the current Stage or for the project.
    - Class 3 changes are those which could be done within the Tolerances of the Stage and the project.

20. Although Class 3 changes **can** be implemented without reference to the Project Board, a Project Manager should be wary of doing so. A Stage which is comfortably within its Tolerances today may find itself at the limit of them next week. Project Boards are not normally sympathetic to cries of "But in the past I've done all these things without charging you", especially if you have a User/*Customer*/supplier relationship. Unless the changes are **very** trivial, it is best to lump these changes together and deal with them in the same way as Classes 1 and 2 (see the next points).

21. Assessed RFCs are returned to the Project Manager to review. If satisfied, they are then passed to the Senior User/*Customer*, who is responsible for putting them into a prioritised list and sounding out other Project Board members on the action to be taken. This action may be to implement, reject, delay decision or defer the request to a later enhancement project.

22. The Project Board's informal decisions are now returned to the Project Manager. Class 1 and 2 changes must cause an unplanned Mid Stage Assessment for the Project Board to formally approve. They should be accompanied by an Exception Report/Plan showing the extra work which would be required during the current Stage towards implementing the changes. It may be that later Stages will also include some of the work, but that will appear in those Stage Plans.

Project Assurance Function

114

General

23. The Team Manager is responsible for scheduling all RFC and O-SR work.
24. The filed master should be updated with the Project Board's decision and the originator informed.
25. The Project Manager should review the meetings of the Team Manager and the relevant members of the Project Assurance Function to ensure that they are occurring with sufficient frequency to cope with the volume of PIs being raised.

Project Assurance Function

EXAMPLE AGENDA FOR AN UNPLANNED MID-STAGE ASSESSMENT

1. Explanation of the reason for the Exception Report.

2. Forecast of the impact of the Exception Report on the Stage and the project.

3. An explanation of the options investigated.

4. Project Board decision. To commission an exception plan or not.

Second meeting or additional items on first meeting agenda

1. The Exception Plan.

2. Project Manager and members of staff with a role in the Project Assurance Function recommendations.

3. Action plan for the revision of the Project Brief and Project Initiation Document.

4. Project Board Decision.

Project Assurance Function

116

EXAMPLE OF MID-STAGE ASSESSMENT MEMO

MEMO

To: The Project Board
        Ace Plumbing Supplies Ltd.

From: Jan McClelland   Project Manager

Subject: Mid-Stage Assessment

Introduction

This paper summarises the reports, presentations and agreements made at the Mid-Stage Assessment held at your offices on the 9th August.

Review of Stage Status

Project Managers Reported that the Stage was still within the original Stage Plan although a number of amendments have been made to the plan. These had been required due to freezing of the User/*Customer* Specification at the previous End-Stage Assessment. These changes had been concerned with the removal of Product 11 (Updated User/*Customer* Specification Report). The first version prototype (Product 7) had been accepted with only one minor change required. The Project Manager thanked the Senior User/*Customer* for the preparatory work they had undertaken with the staff that had enabled this prototype to have been such a success.

Quality Reviews Results

The Project Support Assistant reported that all the Quality Reviews scheduled for the Stage had been completed and only one Product had remedial work still outstanding.

Project Assurance Function

117

The member of the Project Assurance Function responsible for Specialist Supplier Aspects reported that the Project Team had decided to make use of the Product Descriptions from the SSADM manual to supply some of the standards required for the quality criteria. In respect of the standards used for project management he had been asked by several of the User/*Customer*s for an up to date picture of the current state of the project.

This he had done through a verbal briefing which had followed the cascade briefing held by the stock department manager last week.

The member of the Project Assurance Function responsible for Specialist Supplier Aspects is to attend four reviews in this Stage (Products 3,5,8).

Review of Project Status

The Project Manager reported that the project was within the overall Project Plan and that since the User/*Customer* specification had been agreed the level of uncertainty associated with the project had been considerably reduced.

The Project Manager reported that the stock control clerk had written to her with some additional benefits that had been identified. The Project Board asked that the Project Manager include this information in the update to the Business Case at the End-Stage Assessment.

Business Risk Assessment

The Project Manager reported effectiveness of the risk containment strategy. It had (so far) worked well. The only aspect of the risks for the project that was still causing concern was that the development work was dependent on the new version of the operating system that was due for release in September. The Project Manager reported that she had written to the software company and they had confirmed that subject to the completion of the tests it would be available on target.

Project Issue Status

The Project Manager reported that two Project Issues had been received and were being processed. They were both Requests for Change and centered on the physical size of the computers that were to be installed.

Project Assurance Function

118

Forecast For the rest of the Stage

The Project Manager reported that she expected the Stage to be completed on schedule if not a little in advance as there were some Products which would require less work than anticipated due to the frozen User/*Customer* specification.

Review of Stage Tolerance

It was agreed that no review of the Tolerance for this Stage was needed.

Review of Security Policy Arrangements

On advice from the Project Manager and the member of the Project Assurance Function responsible for Specialist Supplier Aspects, the Project Board agreed that no amendments to the security policy were required.

Early start to next Stage

The Project Manager requested that if she did manage to complete this Stage up to five days ahead of schedule then the Project Board agreed that this can be done providing it does not compromise the Business or Technical integrity of the project and that the next Stage Plan is sent to them for comments prior to any work commencing.

Project Assurance Function

The member of the Project Assurance Function responsible for User/*Customer* Aspects was concerned with the number of User/*Customer* Products in the next Stage and felt that it may put a heavy workload on her. The Senior User/*Customer* agreed that she could spend more time on the project if it became necessary up to a maximum of 16 hours per week.

Approval to proceed

The Project Board gave formal approval for the Project Manager to continue with the Stage.

Project Assurance Function

119

SUMMARY OF AN EXCEPTION REPORT AND PLAN

EXCEPTION REPORT		From:	To:
Why This Report is Needed			

PRODUCTS AFFECTED IN THIS STAGE					
Product ID	**Due to Start**	**Due to Finish**	**Impact of Problem**		
			Time	**Cost**	**Comments**

OTHER PRODUCTS/PROJECTS AFFECTED					
Product ID	**Due to Start**	**Due to Finish**	**Impact of Problem**		
			Time	**Cost**	**Comments**

OPTIONS CONSIDERED	**Effect on Problem**	**COST**		**Comments**
		Time	**Resources**	
1.				
2.				
3.				

RECOMMENDATION AND REASONS:

Project Assurance Function

120

EXAMPLE COMPLETED CHECKPOINT REPORT

CHECKPOINT REPORT					
From: *Colin Bloggs*		To: *David Marsh*		For period: *w/c 12/7/98*	
Product ID	**Product Name**	**Due to Start**	**Actual Start**	**Due to Cmplte**	**Actual Cmpltn**
10.01.03.02	Draft Building Requirements Report (1)	13/7/98	12/7/98	15/7/98	15/7/98
11.03.01	Quality Review Invitation	12/7/98	12/7/98	12/7/98	12/7/98
12.02.03	User/*Customer* Acceptance Note for Product 10.01.01.02	12/7/98	12/7/98	13/7/98	13/7/98
15.01.02	Training Plan	14/7/98	14/7/98	15/7/98	15/7/98
16.02.01	Building Permission letter	15/7/98	14/7/98	20/7/98	
10.01.03.03	User/Customer Approval of Building Requirements	16/7/98	15/7/98	21/7/98	

Project Assurance Function

121

EXAMPLE COMPLETED HIGHLIGHT REPORT

HIGHLIGHT REPORT				
From: David Marsh	**To:** Jan McClelland		**For period:** July 1998	

ID No	Product Name	Due to complete	Actual completion	Comments
10	Building Requirements Report	21/7/98	20/7/98	
11	Quality Review	23/7/98	22/7/98	Reviewer on holiday (unplanned)
12	User/*Customer* Acceptance of Building requirements	26/7/98	27/7/98	
13	Building Regulations application	16/7/98	15/7/98	
14	Equipment Order	9/7/98	7/7/98	Found a short cut in procedures
15	Training Courses	27/7/98	23/7/98	Able to use previous course materials
16	Data Collection	20/7/98	26/7/98	New data requirement identified

Variances Analysis			Max	Min	Av	Comments
		% Resources	+ 25% Product 16	-10% Product 15	+4%	
Product Production		**% Cost**	+18%	-9%	+1%	
		% Delay	+30%	-20%	+2%	

Problems/Opportunities Encountered
New data requirements identified in Product 16 - leading to a delay in Product 16.

Impact on Rest of Stage/Product

Problem/extra work from Product 16 will mean that the data conversion (Product 22) will take 20% longer. Impact on Project +5 days on that Stage. Total Tolerance now used is +21 days out of the allowed 30. No action needed as yet.

Project Assurance Function

EXAMPLE OF A METRICS COLLECTION FORM

METRICS COLLECTION FORM			Project:
Product ID	**Product Name**	**Resources Used**	**Comments**

Project Assurance Function

123

6   MANAGING STAGE BOUNDARIES

6.1   Objectives of the Process

This process ensures that at the end of each Stage all the necessary plans and other project management documents are updated and so that the Project Board can make the decision about whether to proceed or not with the next Stage of the project on the most up to date information available.

Projects are divided into Stages for two main reasons.

The first of these is to respect the concept of the planning horizon. Even with the most sophisticated Project Support Infrastructure it is not possible to be confident that the Project Plan accurately represents what has to be done. This because when planning you can only see in detail a limited number of weeks ahead - "the planning horizon". The distance of that horizon in most projects is relatively short - typically 6 weeks or so. Anything beyond that is over the horizon or guess work. Therefore by dividing the project into Stages - which relate to the planning horizon the Project Manager can plan in detail only when the new horizon becomes apparent. Therefore although the whole project is planned (at high level) the really detailed planning is only done just before each Stage starts. Thus the Project Board and Project Manager decide whether the project should proceed to the next Stage when they have the most accurate and up to date view of the next 6 weeks or so. They make the decision to proceed or not on how well the Stage Plan matches that of the overall Project Plan.

The second reason for using Stages relates to the concept of the "Cone of Uncertainty".

Project Assurance Function

124

This analogy means that at the start of the project the widest part of the cone is encountered - maximum amounts of uncertainty. As development work is undertaken and the project moves towards the narrow end of the cone the amount of uncertainty reduces. So as the project moves forward the Project Manager and Project Board update the project documentation and plans to reflect this reduced uncertainty.

This re-documentation is carried out at convenient points in time corresponding with the completion of a Work package or major Product or Products and thus when they have narrowed the uncertainty. These points are the end of Stages. This reduction in uncertainty together with the confidence that the next Stage plan conforms (within acceptable limits) to the Project Plan means that they can authorise the next Stage to commence and the project to continue.

The objectives of the process are to ensure that:

- sufficient up to date information is provided to the Project Board to enable them to allow the next Stage to start and the project to continue;

- to close the work completed in the previous Stage and to ensure that all the Products that were planned to be delivered have been completed or acceptable reasons provided for why they were not;

- to record any lessons learnt for future use in this project, or in others;

- to formally agree the plan for the next Stage of the project, and set the Tolerance for the expenditure of resources in its delivery.

Project Assurance Function

6.2   Description of the Process

The Project Manager assisted by the members of the Project Assurance Function review the content of the Project Management Documents to ensure that they are still valid. Particular attention is paid to the:

- Terms of Reference for the project (Project Brief and or Mandate) - particularly its objectives scope and constraints;
- Project Management Team design;
- appointments made to the Project Management Team;
- Products planned to be developed in the next Stage;
- Product Descriptions of these Products.

These are re-evaluated to see if they need to be updated or changed. All such changes are subject to the approval of the Project Board.

Having completed this re-evaluation the Project Manager then prepare the Stage Plan. This includes developing any new or modified Products Descriptions - preparing detailed and individual plan as required. On completion of these plans the Project Manager must compare them with the original Project Plan and any difference must be investigated. The Project Manager then updates all the other relevant project documentation to reflect the increased knowledge about the project that has been acquired during the previous Stage and the planning for the next. The Project Manager must make the preparation for the End Stage Assessment - start of the next Stage (including the development of a report on the previous Stage).

If in preparing this report it is apparent that the project is not meeting or has not met either its delivery of Products or over spent its resource usage target or budget then the Project Manager must prepare an Exception Report/Plan for consideration by the Project Board.

Project Assurance Function

126

This Report/Plan must give a full description of what has happened, an analysis of the reasons for the problems and suggested solutions.

This report is considered by the Project Board at the End of Stage Assessment - together with the Project Manager's End of Stage Report and appropriate action taken.

6.3 Outputs to be Produced by this Process

- SB1.   Stage Plan

- SB2   Updated Project Plan

- SB3   Updated Business Case

- SB4   Updated Risk Log

- SB5   Stage End Report

- SB6   As required - Exception Plan

- SB7   As required- Updates to the Project Initiation
         Document and Project Brief

Project Assurance Function

127

6.4   Checklist

A   Review and offer constructive criticism on End-Stage Report produced by the Project and team Manager. This report typically includes:

- a report on any problems with developing the Products in the Stage;
- an evaluation of any lessons learned in producing the User/*Customer* and Specialist Supplier Products during the Stage and any impact that this may have on the rest of the project;
- a report on the investigation of any problems. In particular attention should be paid to any problem that occurred with the definition and accuracy of the Product Descriptions and Quality Criteria;
- a report which compares the planned and actual progress in meeting the User/*Customer* needs.

B   Brief the relevant members of the Project Board with your view of the current situation and the overall progress of the project.

C   Assist the Project and Team Manager with the completion of the plans and Product Descriptions for the next Stage of the project.

D   Ensure the Project Initiation Document is updated to reflect any changes to the project agreed during the Stage. In particular the members of the Project Assurance Function should check for any changes in User/*Customer* organisation, scope or requirements, the Business Case and Risk Assessment.

Project Assurance Function

E   With the Project and Team Manager prepare Product Descriptions for the Products in this Stage and the associated Stage. Attend a meeting for the Project Manager, Team Manager and the members of the Project Assurance Function to agree:

- that the Stage Plan includes all the required Work Packages or Products;
- the content of each User/*Customer* and Specialist Supplier Product Description and its accompanying Quality Criteria;
- which Products will need to be Quality Reviewed and what method of review is required;
- who the Chairman and Reviewers will be for each of the formal Product Quality Reviews;
- which of the Stage's Work Packages or Products have links with others;
- the content and format of the Stage Plan and that it includes all the resources needed to produce and review the Work Packages or Products;
- which Work Packages or Products will need formal approval by the organisation and who should sign the acceptance memo.

F   Ensure all the User/*Customer* and Specialist Supplier staff involved in this Stage:

- are aware of what is required of them;
- are able to carry out the task allocated;
- understand their role in the project.

G   Ensure that the agreed Product Description have been filed correctly.

Project Assurance Function

129

H   Ensure you receive from the Project Support Assistant a list of the Products that are to be developed in this Stage.

I   Ensure you receive from the Project Support Assistant a list of all the dates and types of progress reports to be provided during the Stage.

6.5 Guidance Notes

A   At the end of each Stage the Project Board formally review that Stage and accept it (by signing the End-Stage Report). They also review the Project Brief and the Project Initiation Document to ensure they are still valid before allowing the Project Manager to start the next Stage.

[Note: Although this assessment and review must be carried out before the start of the next Stage it is quite normal for work on the Stage to have already commenced. This overlap is only allowed at the Project Manager's discretion and must have been accepted in principle by the Project Board. If the Project Manager feels there is a real doubt that the project will be allowed to proceed then the standard procedure should be used.]

The End-Stage Report contains:

- a progress report on the Stage;
- an evaluation of the impact of anything that has arisen during the Stage;
- an evaluation on the remainder of the project of anything that has arisen during the Stage;
- any amendment/addendum to the Project Initiation Document agreed or identified as being required during the Stage;
- a report which compares the resources used with those budgeted/agreed for the Stage;
- Project Assurance Function activities during the Stage;
- Project/Team Management activities during the Stage.

Project Assurance Function

This report is usually an amalgam of the inputs from the Project and Team Managers and the members of the Project Assurance Function.

The members of the Project Assurance Function must discuss and agree the content of the report and Assessment with the Project and Team Managers before it is circulated to the Project Board.

The members of the Project Assurance Function review the report produced by the Project and Team Manager

If any member of the Project Assurance Function does not agree with the Project and Team Manager's assessment of the Stage or the project then a separate report must be prepared and the Project Board informed about this situation. **This does not occur very often - when it does it is a serious problem and must be investigated by the Project Board.**

The format and content of the End Stage Report will have been described in the Project Initiation Document.

B   Brief the relevant member of the Project Board on your view of the Stage and the progress of the project.

The Project Board will review the End Stage Report so it is advisable to include in your discussion with the relevant member your view of the assessment, its contents, and any action you consider is required by the Project Board.

Project Assurance Function

[Note: Be careful what you raise with the Project Board. Remember they are managing the direction of the project and ensuring the required resources are available - not the technical management. If there are any technical matters that need to be discussed the Project Board are more concerned with the impact of these issues on the project not the issues themselves.]

C   The members of the Project Assurance Function responsible for User/*Customer* and Specialist Supplier aspects should assist the Project and Team Manager to prepare and finalise the Product Descriptions and Plan for the next Stage.

D   The members of the Project Assurance Function together with the Project Manager should review and update the Project Initiation Document.   In particular it should be amended to reflect any changes and amendments agreed by the Project Board during the Stage and be re-submitted to them for agreement.   They should also validate that the project is still within its agreed Project Brief.

The members of the Project Assurance Function responsible for User/*Customer* and Specialist Supplier aspects must ensure that the Project and Team Managers update the Risk Assessment and the Business Case to reflect what has occurred in the Stage.

E   Introduction

The amount of time required for your contribution to the Stage Plan can be considerable - so please do ensure that before starting the process you have assessed the amount of your time required.

It is important to have completed this process prior to the start of the next Stage.

Project Assurance Function

Ideally work on the Stage Plan should start immediately after the half-way point of the previous Stage. This process will require a number of meetings between the Project and Team Manager and the members of the Project Assurance Function.

The Stage Level Plan consists of:

- Product Flow Diagram;
- Product Breakdown Structure;
- A Gantt or Bar Chart;
- A Resource Spreadsheet;
- Product Descriptions and Quality Criteria;
- Accompanying notes (Plan Text).

[Note: This section of the guidelines only covers Product Flow Diagrams, Product Descriptions and Product Breakdown Structures. For guidance on the production of Project and Stage plan, and the accompanying Plan Text see the PRINCE manual.]

The Stage Level Product Flow Diagram must show all the Products or Work Packages to be produced in this Stage.

What is a Work Package ?

Something which represents a significant block of related activities or Products e.g. the initial design of the building, a set of cost or materials estimates.

Project Assurance Function

How big is a Work Package?

This depends on the project and the frequency/method of monitoring the development or progress of the project. The size of a Work Package is best described in terms of staff days of effort needed to produce it or the number of Products it contains. In most projects it is not normal to use the concept of a Work Package unless it contains at least three Products each requiring more than five man days effort.

What is a Product?

Something which represents a completed activity or block of work e.g. a document or piece of a computer programme or screen design.

How big is a Product?

This depends on the project and the frequency/method of monitoring the development or progress of the project. The size of a Product is best described in terms of staff days of effort needed to produce it. In most projects it is not normally required to identify Products with less than three to five man days effort.

How do you check a Product Description?

To check a Product Description you must ensure that it describes what is required - in particular the format and contents of the Product.

Be realistic - do not overspecify the Product. If in doubt test the description as follows:

- could I produce what is required from this description?
- could the person allocated to this Product do so from the description?
- does this Product feed into any other Products or Work Package - if so will it provide them with what they will need?

To check the Quality Criteria ensure they exhibit these characteristics:

- they are clear and unambiguous;
- when you test against them the answer is either yes or no;
- they been prioritised to reflect the importance of this Product in this project.

It is helpful when checking the criteria to find out who produced them, and if they have been used before. You should carefully check any which are being used for the first time or were produced by someone who is not experienced.

If you are not happy with the criteria then you should research and propose amendments, either based on your knowledge, or find someone in the organisation who can help you. The Project and Team Managers and the rest of the Project Assurance Function must be kept in the picture about the revisions you consider should be made.

[Remember: The purpose of agreeing the Product Description and Quality Criteria before the Product is produced is to 'get it right first time'. A few days delay to ensure the Product Descriptions are correct will prevent much wasted effort and confusion.]

i) When de-composing the Project Level Products into Stage Level Products the three types of Products used in a PRINCE project, Specialist Supplier, Management and Quality, must be included. I recommend you include a fourth category that of Communication Products - these include such things as the Communication Strategy for the project, User/*Customer* and organisational briefings etc.

Members of the Project Assurance Function must agree that all the required Work Packages or Products are contained in the Stage Plan. Each of the members of the Project Assurance Function should ensure that the Products for which they have responsibility are both correct and have been agreed by the members of the organisation they represent.

Particular attention should be paid by the User/*Customer* member of the Project Assurance Function to ensure that User/*Customer* education and training Products are included early enough in the project to help enable them to participate fully in the development of the project.

The member of the Project Assurance Function responsible for the Specialist Supplier aspects will need to concentrate on ensuring that all the Specialist Supplier Products required are included in the Stage Plan and also the lessons learnt and any knowledge and experiences from previous projects are incorporated into the plan.

Project Assurance Function

137

The Project Support Assistant must involve both the User/*Customer* and the Specialist Supplier members of the Project Assurance Function in the agreement of the Stage Plan. They should both involve other people in the organisation with relevant experience or knowledge to help them assure that the Stage Plan is both appropriate and complete.

ii) Following on from the identification of the Stage Products it will be necessary to produce Product Descriptions for each of them. These descriptions can be developed by any combination of the Project Support Office, Project Manager, Team Manager and Project Assurance Function. What is important is that the members of the Project Assurance Function discuss and agree the content of the Specialist Supplier and User/*Customer* Product Descriptions and accompanying Quality Criteria with the parts of the organisation they represent.

This will help to ensure that knowledge of the project is spread throughout the organisation. Any comments or questions raised during this process must be resolved prior to the start of the development of the Products.

iii) As with the Project Level Plans not all the Stage Products need the rigour, or expense of, a formal Quality Review.

It is important to identify those Products which have a political as well as a User/*Customer* or other significance because these will need a formal Quality Review.

It is recommended that guidelines are drawn up to identify any such Products (see the Project Initiation section of this document). In addition you can use the 'so what' test.

Project Assurance Function

Question - If I don't formally Quality Review this Product - THEN - so what?

If the answer causes concern i.e. it may have consequences on the project's development, then the Product should be formally Quality Reviewed.

A similar process to that used in the preparation of the Project Initiation Document should be used to ensure the Project Assurance Function agree which Products will be formally or informally Quality Reviewed.

iv) The Project Assurance Function should ensure that for each Product to be formally Quality Reviewed the Chairman and Reviewers have been identified.

The Chairman could be either:

- the Project Support Assistant or the PAF (Business);
- a senior member of the organisation who understands the Product;
- a nominee from an independent source.

It is important to select a Chairman who:

- can fulfil the role effectively;
- will be impartial and not get personally involved;
- can allocate the time to the role;
- understand his/her role in the PRINCE Quality Review procedures.

The Reviewers typically come from either:

- the Project Assurance Function;
- other departments in the organisation;
- from outside the organisation.

It is important to select reviewers who :

- have time available to fulfil the role;
- are competent and will be conscientious in reviewing the Product;
- understand or have been trained in the PRINCE Quality Review procedures;
- are recognised as being technically competent and empowered by the organisation to review the Product.

v) Examine each of the Product Descriptions to identify which Products link together. This linkage can be within the Stage, to other Products in the Work Package or another Stage of the project, or to other projects.

Pay particular attention to the Products that are produced in this Stage which will become incorporated into other Products later in this project or another project. These Product Descriptions should be examined by the Project Assurance Function and the Project Manager to ensure that the Products will successfully link. Particular attention must be given to the Quality Criteria of such Products to ensure that any prioritisation (of the Quality Criteria) has not affected the compatibility of that Product with others.

Project Assurance Function

vi) The Stage Level Product Flow Diagram will enable the Project and Team Managers and the Project Assurance Function to develop the Project and Stage Plans. Your involvement in this process will be contained in the job description and the Terms of Reference agreed with you at the start of the project.

vii) One of the main reasons for an organisation using the PRINCE project management method is that it enables the end User/*Customer*s of the project to become involved in its development. The User/*Customer*s must decide whether the Products produced are acceptable or not. These decisions should, as far as possible, be taken by the members of the organisation and not the Project Board or development team. This ensures that the project becomes the property of the organisation and not the Project Team's.

To help achieve this involvement the member of the Project Assurance Function responsible for the User/*Customer* aspects must ensure that, where appropriate, acceptance of the Products produced are taken by the representatives of the organisation.

This process is shown in the Stage Plan by the acceptance Product. So for example a Stage Plan should show three sub-Products for each Product:

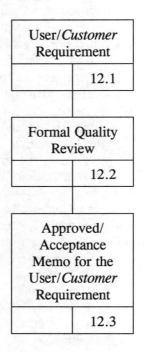

User/*Customer* Requirement	
	12.1

Formal Quality Review	
	12.2

Approved/ Acceptance Memo for the User/*Customer* Requirement	
	12.3

The members of the Project Assurance Function should assist the Project and Team Managers to identify who should approve these products by recommending which members of staff should approve the Product and sign the acceptance memo shown in the diagram.

Project Assurance Function

142

[Note: It is sometimes possible to combine the Quality Review and the decision making process but only do so if you are sure that they can/should be carried out by the same people.]

Choose approvers who have the:

- right level of authority;
- right level of knowledge;
- confidence of the organisation to make that decision.

[Note: Sometimes these people may also have a role as a member of the Project Board. It is vital that they understand they are approving the Product on behalf of the organisation and not as a member of the Project Board.]

The normal consultative processes needed to get the involvement of these decision makers is not part of the various PRINCE procedures and systems. You will need to write to or talk to them to ensure that they are aware of, and able to, carry out this role.

F   The members of the Project Assurance Function responsible for User/*Customer* and Specialist Supplier aspects and the Project Manager should ensure that the staff who will be involved in this Stage as Quality Reviewers, or Product approvers understand their role and have the required skills.

The members of the Project Assurance Function can help the Project Manager to provide the User/*Customer* and Specialist Supplier staff with any required training or coaching.

If such training needs are identified then the members of the Project Assurance Function are expected to play a major role in the supply of any advice and training.

Project Assurance Function

G   The agreed Product Descriptions and Quality Criteria will be input into the Stage filing system by the Project and Team Manager.

The members of the Project Assurance Function should check that a copy of each Product Descriptions has been received.

H   The Stage Plan contains a considerable amount of detail and it is usual for the Project Support Assistant to produce a checklist or schedule which specifically shows the Product delivery and Quality Review arrangements.   The members of the Project Assurance Function should ensure that they receive a copy of the schedule.

I   In a similar format to that of the Product and Quality Review schedules the Project Support Assistant should produce a schedule of the Checkpoint and Highlight Reports to be produced.   As with other schedules the Project Support Assistant must ensure that these are distributed to the appropriate people, including the members of the Project Assurance Function.

6.6   Supporting Documents

1. Example of an Agenda for an End-Stage Assessment.

2. Example of an End-Stage Report and memo.

3. Example of a Product Checklist.

4. Example of a Progress Report Checklist.

Project Assurance Function

EXAMPLE AGENDA FOR END-STAGE ASSESSMENT

1. Project Manager's Report on the previous Stage.

2. Project Assurance Function Report on the previous Stage.

3. Quality Reviews - Statistics and results.

4. Project Issue - Statistics and results.

5. Standards - project management method and standards.

6. The Project Plan - An update.

7. The Business Case - An update.

8. Risk Assessment and containment strategy - An update.

9. Next Stage Plan and Tolerance.

10. Updates to the Project Initiation Document and approval to proceed.

Project Assurance Function

EXAMPLE OF END-STAGE ASSESSMENT MEMO

M E M O

To: The Project Board
        Ace Plumbing Supplies Ltd.

From: Jan McClelland   Project Manager

Subject: End-Stage Assessment

Introduction

This paper summarises the reports, presentations and agreements made at the End-Stage Assessment Meeting held at your offices on the 30th August.

Project Managers Report

The project was still within the original Project Brief although a number of amendments have been made to the Project Initiation Document. These have been approved by the Project Board and are included in the current version (number 4) of the Project Initiation Document.

The major uncertainty left in the project was the conversion of the existing stock and sales records. To reduce this uncertainty the Project Manager requested that some of the staff were asked to assist the team who were to key in the data into the data base during September. The Senior User/*Customer* agreed to arrange this and the Project Plan is to be amended by the Project Support Assistant to reflect the increase in User/*Customer* involvement.

Project Assurance Function Report

User/*Customer* Aspects

The only item raised by the member of the Project Assurance Function responsible for User/*Customer* Aspects was concerned with the number of Product Descriptions that she had been asked to review for the next Stage.

Project Assurance Function

146

The Project Manager had explained that this was an exceptional Stage as it had contained a lot more User/*Customer* Products than previous Stages and this had resulted in the member of the Project Assurance Function responsible for User/*Customer* Aspects having to vet approximately 20 Product Descriptions in the last three weeks. It was agreed that if the Project Manager saw that such a workload was likely to occur again then she would ask the Project Board to appoint a further person to the Project Assurance Function User/*Customer* Aspects to help out.

Quality Reviews

The Project Support Assistant reported that all the Quality Reviews scheduled for the Stage had been completed and only two Products had remedial work still outstanding. The member of the Project Assurance Function responsible for Specialist Supplier Aspects who attended the review of Product 3 said that he felt that it could have been reviewed informally. He had examined the records to see why it had been selected for a formal review and it appears as if the checklist of the factors for selecting formal versus informal reviews had not been correctly applied by the Team Manager. The Project Board asked the Project Manager to review the agreed level of review for the next Stage of the project to ensure that the checklist was being correctly applied and that it did reflect the needs of this project.

Project Issue Status

The Configuration Librarian reported that three Project Issues had been received and had all been processed. The Project Board asked the Project Support Assistant and the Project Manager for an analysis of all the Project Issues received to date to see if any trends were emerging.

Standards

The member of the Project Assurance Function responsible for Specialist Supplier Aspects reported that the use of the Product Descriptions from the SSADM manual had helped in setting the standards required in the quality criteria. In respect of the standards used for project management it had been requested by several of the User/*Customers* for the distribution of the Highlight Report to be amended to include them. It was agreed by the Project Board to amend the distribution list to include these people.

Project Assurance Function

The Project Plan

The Project Manager gave a short presentation on the changes to the Project Plan since it was last approved (Version 5). The only changes were that the data conversion and take on Products had been allocated additional User/*Customer* resources (see item 2).

The Project Board approved the plan but pointed out that as there was only 13 days Tolerance left any further time slippage would resort in them having to request additional time from the main board of Ace Plumbing. The Project Manager agreed to ensure that Project Board was informed if she felt that it would go outside of the remaining Tolerance.

The Business Case

The Project Manager and the member of the Project Assurance Function responsible for Business Aspects have updated the Business Case to reflect the costs incurred to date and also the updated benefits that were identified during the last Stage. The Project Board asked the Senior User/*Customer* to investigate the claimed increased benefits and report on this at the next Mid-Stage Assessment.

Business Risk Assessment

The Project Manager reported on the risk assessment review that had been carried out. There were no new risks identified and the containment strategy had worked well. The overall level of risk for the project was still medium due to the development work being dependent on the new version of the operating system that was due for release in September.

Next Stage Plan

The Project Manager presented the next Stage Plan and explained that it was different from that in version 4 of the Project Plan as follows:

Product 12 was no longer required due to the User/*Customer* specification being frozen by the Project Board at the last End-Stage Assessment. Total duration of the Stage is less three days and the resources required less 24 man days. A new Product has been identified as being required this is shown as Product 97. It is a trial of the data conversion software that will be carried out in this Stage to identify any problems that may arise when the full conversion takes place.

Project Assurance Function

148

The member of the Project Assurance Function responsible for Business Aspects reported that the changes in this plan from the Project Plan had been included in both the updated risk assessment and Business Case. The members of the Project Assurance Function then made a short presentation on their view of the next Stage of the project. They had no additional comments except that they felt the inclusion of Product 97 would help the project.

The Project Board gave formal approval for the project to proceed with the next Stage.

Project Assurance Function

EXAMPLE OF PRODUCT CHECKLIST

PRODUCT CHECKLIST				For period:	
Product Name	Start Date	Finish Date	Developers	Resources Agreed	Costs Agreed

Project Assurance Function

EXAMPLE OF PROGRESS REPORTING CHECKLIST

PROGRESS REPORTING CHECKLIST				For period:	
Type of Report	From:	To:	Date Due	Format Standard Reference	Date Completed

Project Assurance Function

151

7 PROJECT CLOSURE

7.1 Objectives of the Process

One of the factors used to determine whether a group of activities constitute a project or not is the concept that all projects have a finite end. Whilst in a majority of cases this is so the term project can also be used to denote activities that are on going for example a homeless persons housing project. The PRINCE methods - both one and two work on the assumption that all projects are of the former type i.e. a definite end point. This process is used to ensure that these sorts of projects are shut down effectively and the lessons learnt are captured for reuse on future projects. Failure to have this formal shut down process results in organisations not tasking operational management to take over responsibility for the changes that have been made to the organisations operational infrastructure, the project team never disbanded and in extreme cases the project never really being regarded as closed.

If the project is never really closed than it is very common for the organisation not to realise the benefits the project was designed to achieve as it is not aware that the project has been delivered. If this occurs then the organisation is also denied the opportunity to take stock of the new situation, to record the experience gained and to declare what goals have been achieved and those that remain or were discovered during the project itself.

In addition to the two types of projects previously identified a third group has emerged recently where the Project Board are kept on as a continual review board. In such cases they are typically renamed System Development Board and are responsible for seeing that the deliverable produced by the project continue to provide the business benefits that were the reason for its commissioning.

Project Assurance Function

In addition this board monitors the performance of the new infrastructure and acts as the co-ordinating body for any enhancement or change requests.

In such cases the Closing a Project process should still be carried out but modified to take account of the formation of such a board and the responsibilities that they will have.

As with all of the PRINCE processes this one must be tailored to meet the specific requirements of the organisation and the type and nature of the project.

The objectives of the process are to ensure that:

- the organisation has the opportunity to review whether the aims and objectives of the project have been achieved;

- the User/*Customer* or organisation are asked to confirm that the development team have fulfilled there obligations as defined in the Project Initiation Document;

- to receive confirmation from the User/*Customer* or the organisation that all the expected Products have been delivered and are of the required quality;

- that all the procedures and systems needed to support the Products and system that has been delivered are in place and operating satisfactorily;

- any follow on action, or uncompleted Products, or on going Project Issues have been documented and assigned to relevant members of the organisation;

Project Assurance Function

153

- that any experiences gained or lessons learnt are documented for future reference;

[Note: This particular objective is especially important in those projects that have ended prematurely for example if an insurmountable problem has emerged.]

- that arrangements for the Post Implementation Evaluation or Review of the project and the benefits it was to provide have been put into place;

- to notify all members of the Project Team and associated projects and programmes of the formal disbanding of the project and the transition arrangements that have been put into place to transfer responsibility to the relevant operational area.

Without these elements being in place the organisation cannot ensure that the project closes within a managed and controlled framework.

7.2 Description of the Process

The process covers all the work carried out by the Project Board, Project Manager, Project Support and Project Assurance Function to formally close the project and to inform the relevant parties of the closure.

The process includes checking that the requirements of the Project Mandate, Project Brief and Project Initiation Document have been fulfilled or identifying any differences or variations.

Project Assurance Function

The Project Issue and Risk Logs are also examined to identify any outstanding issues or risks that need to be handed over either to the maintenance and operational teams or to any enhancement or maintenance project that is likely to be commissioned. The Project Manager should inspect the Risk Log particularly carefully to identify those countermeasures or containment strategies that either worked well or were ineffective and ensure that attention to these are drawn in either the End of Project Report or the Lessons Learnt Report.

In addition the Project Manager closely examines the original and revised plan to identify as above any discrepancies or variations that occurred.

The findings of these examinations are discussed with the Project Support Office and the Project Assurance Function and the combined views documented in the End of Project Report.

The Project Manager also now summarises all the entries in the Lessons Learnt log into the End of Project Lessons and Learnt Report. The Project Manager should identify both positive and negative lessons. Particular attention must be paid to any of the standard or common processes or practices used by other projects.

In addition the Project Manager must prepare for the Project Board or others the required letters or memos of notification of the close of the project- including (if relevant) the User/*Customer* or owner of the project the Programme Manager and the Programme Executive Board.

7.3   Outputs to be Produced by this Process

- CP1   De-commissioning a Project Report.

- CP2   Follow-on Actions Report.

- CP3   A Project Evaluation Project

7.4   Checklist

A   Review the End of Project Report prepared by the Project Manager.

B   Confirm with the Project Support Assistant that all Project Issues referring to User/*Customer* and Specialist Supplier Products have reached an acceptable status.

C   Ensure that formal Product acceptance exists for all the Products planned to be accepted by the User/*Customer* and Specialist Supplier community.

D   Confirm that the relevant member of the Project Board has signed the Project Closure and Acceptance Letters.

E   Assist the Project Manager to informally discuss the End of Project Report with the relevant members of the Project Board.

F   Assist the Project Manager and the remainder of the Project Assurance Function to agree:

- the proposed date for the Post Implementation Review;

- the proposed date for the Security, Backup and Contingency Procedures Review.

[Note : the last item is not always required]

G   Assist the Project Manager with the Project Closure Meeting.

7.5   Guidance Notes

A   The Project Manager must convene a meeting with the members of the Project Assurance Function to discuss what should be included in the End of Project Report. This report should be reviewed by the members of the Project Assurance Function.

In addition you should jointly agree any recommendations you intend to make to the Project Board about actions needed to implement lessons learned in this project. These may be of either general importance or specific to this project. You will be particularly concerned with lessons learned about the User/*Customer* involvement throughout the project. Mention good points as well as bad ones.

B   All Project Issues must be closed by the end of the project. They will either have been answered fully or converted into Requests For Change or Off-Specification Reports. The latter two types of Project Issues must have reached an acceptable status. This means that they will have been either:

- actioned

- rejected

or

- deferred.

Those deferred should have been prepared for transfer to the after project maintenance team by the Project Support Assistant.

Project Assurance Function

158

The Project Manager will also check that the Project Support Assistant has carried out a final Configuration Audit and that the Configuration Control records are up to date.

You should check on the state of the Configuration Management System by carrying out a short audit on one or more of the Products relevant to your area of responsibility - selected at random.

C   You should check that the Project Support Assistant and the Project Manager have ensured that all the Products for the User/*Customer* and Specialist Supplier communities have been delivered and accepted. A large proportion of the effort needed to check this aspect can be accomplished by checking the Configuration Status Account and supplementing it with a series of spot checks with the Specialist Supplier and User/*Customer* communities to ensure that the status account is accurate.

D   At the successful conclusion of acceptance tests, the Senior User/*Customer* should have prepared and signed a Project Acceptance Letter, signifying on behalf of the User/*Customer* community that it was ready to accept the Work Packages or Products developed by the project. The manager/s responsible for supporting and maintaining the Work Packages or Products delivered by the project should also prepare and sign a Project Acceptance Letter when they are satisfied that the Products delivered by the project can be operated properly.

Because this Manager/s is not normally on the Project Board, both the Senior User/*Customer* and Senior Supplier members of the Project Board are asked to countersign the Project Acceptance Letters. *If that Manager/s is on the Project Board, their signatures are not required on this document.*

Project Assurance Function

159

E   The Project Closure meeting will involve a considerable number of documents. It is advisable for the Project Board members to have been briefed by their respective member of the Project Assurance Function prior to the meeting. This ensures that any necessary research or detailed answers to specific questions are addressed outside the Project Board meeting. The Project Closure meeting will then be both effective and efficient in its use of everyone's time and concentrate on the strategic issues rather than those of a detailed nature. The members of the Project Assurance Function must brief their respective members of the Project Board on the current status of the project, so you should ensure that you allocate some time to this activity.

F   The Project Support Assistant must arrange and prepare for the Project Closure meeting. Remember that it is not always necessary to hold a separate Project Closure meeting. In many projects the Project Closure meeting is combined with the final End-Stage Assessment.

i)   The Project Board must discuss and agree the date and arrangements for the Post implementation Evaluation or Review. The Project Manager will prepare recommendations to the Project Board on the date for the review and who should carry it out.

The members of the Project Assurance Function should review the date chosen to ensure it allows for the full effects of the changes the project is to make to have occurred. Time should be given for the new system to settle down. Typically a full business cycle will have elapsed before the review takes place. The choice of who should carry out the review is not usually solely the responsibility of the Project Manager and Project Board. The Project Board makes a recommendation to the PCA or Programme Board.

Project Assurance Function

160

Typical choices are :

- the Project Manager

  and / or

- the Project Support Assistant

  and/ or

- members of the Project Assurance Function.

ii) It is important to ensure that the Security, Backup and Contingency Arrangements are in place and have been accepted by the relevant members of the organisation. In some projects this may be the responsibility of a specialist department, and therefore not the responsibility of the Project Board. In other projects the need for this aspect of the development to be considered by the Project Board may not occur.

There are a number of factors which might cause this. For example, the system may be contained on an existing IT platform or infrastructure which has its own Security and Backup Systems. In addition, it is advisable for the members of the Project Assurance Function to assist the Project Support Assistant and the Project Manager to recommend a date to the Project Board for a Review of Security, Backup and Contingency Arrangements to be carried out once the newly installed system has become established in the organisation's culture. This review could be timed to coincide with the Post Implementation Review.

Project Assurance Function

G   At the Project Closure meeting a short presentation is made to the Project Board by each member of the Project Assurance Function on each of the major reports to be considered by the Project Board. Asking each member of the Project Assurance Function and the Project Support Assistant to the closure meeting gives the Project Board the opportunity to thank them and recognise the efforts they have made.

The Project Closure Report is best presented by the Project Manager, assisted as required by members of the Project Assurance Function. Particular attention must be given to any recommendations for changes to the general project management method. The reasons for these recommendations should be explained and the Project Board asked to endorse them so that they are included in the End of Project Report to the PCA or Programme Board.

The report on the status of Project Issues can be presented by the Project Support Assistant and the members of the Project Assurance Function. The Project Manager should ensure that any Project Issues which need to be taken forward into an enhancement or further project are pointed out and have the Project Board's endorsement in the End of Project Report.

The report on the handover of deliverables can be given by the relevant members of the Project Assurance Function assisted by the Project Support Assistant as required. The report should concentrate only on any problems or lessons learned and not be a list of who accepted what.

This information should be made available to the Project Board in the form of a checklist which describes the Product, who accepted it and when.

The Project Support Assistant or Project Manager should report on the status of the Project and Stage Files and the procedures to be used to hand over the project documentation to the maintenance and operation departments.

The Project Manager, supported by the Project Assurance Function should formally present to the Project Board the Acceptance Letters from the Specialist Supplier and User/*Customer* communities. The Project Board's attention must be drawn to any codicils added to the letters. The strategic implications of these codicils should be discussed by the Project Board and any recommendations to be made to the PCA or Programme Board, in the End of Project Report, agreed.

The recommended arrangements for the Post Implementation Review and the Security, Backup and Contingency Procedures Review should be proposed by the Project Manager. The Project Board should be asked to put the agreed recommendation in the End of Project Report.

7.6 Supporting Documents

1. Example of a Configuration Status Account

2. Example of a Configuration Audit Checklist

3. Example of a Project Closure Report-Project Manager.

4. Example of a Project Closure Report-Project Assurance Function.

5. Example Agenda for Project Closure Meeting.

Project Assurance Function

EXAMPLE OF A CONFIGURATION STATUS ACCOUNT
Legend
D = Draft; R = Reviewed; A = Approved

FC = Filing Cabinet

CONFIGURATION STATUS ACCOUNT					DATE		
Product ID	10	11	12	13	14	15	16
Product Name	Scrn Des	QR Rpt	Accept Memo	Impl Plan	Equip Ord	Trg Crs	Data Coll
Version Number	2	1	1	3	2	3	1
Author	BH	EP	SLS	BF	JK	SD	TB
Date Completed	20/7	22/7	27/7	15/7	7/7	23/7	26/7
QR Report number	10/02/1	11/01/1	12/01/1	13/03/1	14/02/1	15/03/1	16/01/1
Location	FC1	· FC2	FC3	FC1	FC1	FC1	FC1
Linked Work Packages and or Products	11, 12, 15, 16	10, 12	10, 11	16, 7	4, 5	10,	10, 13
Status	A	A	A	A	A	A	A
Comments							

Project Assurance Function

164

CONFIGURATION AUDIT CHECKLIST

1. Does the information in the Configuration Item Description Records match the physical Product? Check such data as:

   > identifier
   > version number
   > status
   > author
   > title
   > location

2. Does the library contain the latest version of any Product which has reached at least draft status?

3. Does the library contain the master copy of all versions of a Product (including archives)?

4. Does the library hold accurate information on Product copy holders?

5. Are superseded copies being recovered and destroyed?

6. Are there any unofficial Product copies being used?

7. Are Product submission procedures in place, understood by all and being used effectively?

8. Is there a link in the configuration records of a Product version to any Quality Reviews held for it?

9. Do Configuration Item names, identifiers and version numbers meet the standards laid down in the Project Initiation Document?

10. Are Product issue procedures in place, understood by all and used effectively?

11. Is configuration data held in a manner which facilitates its easy control and update by the Configuration Librarian?

Project Assurance Function

165

12. Is the data held in a manner which facilitates the easy Production of information for impact analysis and Configuration Status Accounts?

13. Are external Work Packages and or Products and their source easily identified in the records?

14. Is there an effective method of maintaining up to date information on external Work Packages and or Products? For example, will the Configuration Library be informed of any change to such Work Packages and or Products?

15. Are all Project Issues being logged and identified properly?

16. Are the originators of Project Issues being kept informed of progress at each status change? Is the evaluation of Project Issue being carried out by the Members of staff with a role in the Project Assurance Function correctly and without undue delay?

17. Is the decision process for Project Issues being correctly carried out?

18. Are the Project Issue logs up to date?

19. Is the master of all Project Issues, Requests For Change and Off-Specification Reports held in the appropriate file?

20. Are Requests For Change and Off-Specification Reports being processed correctly according to the standards laid down in the Project Initiation Document?

21. Is a cross-reference maintained in both directions between actioned Project Issues and the affected Configuration Items?

22. Is an actioned Request For Change or Off-Specification Report causing a new Product version to be generated?

23. Are there safeguards to prevent different versions of a Product being under development at the same time - or the same version number being used by different developers simultaneously?

Project Assurance Function

166

EXAMPLE OF A PROJECT CLOSURE REPORT - PROJECT MANAGER

To: The Project Board
                Ace Plumbing Supplies Ltd.

From :   The Project Manager.

Introduction

The stock and sales project has now been completed and this report has been prepared for the Project Board by the Project Manager to provide a summary of the lessons learnt during this project which can then be incorporated into the End Of Project report to the Strategy Group so that the recommendations made can be taken into account in future projects.

This report is divided into six Sections.

Section One	Selection and appointment of the Project Management Team.
Section Two	The involvement of the Project Management Team in planning and controlling the project.
Section Three	The operation of the Quality Review process.
Section Four	The operation of the Project Issue process.
Section Five	Observations on the project management standards and procedures used.
Section Six	Recommendations for consideration for adoption in future projects.

Project Assurance Function

Section One   Selection and appointment of the Project Management Team.

This was rather an unusual project in that it was the first major IT project in this company and the use of a structured approach was new to all of the members of Ace Plumbing Supplies who took roles in this project.

The Project Board were selected by the members of the board except for Specialist Supplier Aspects member who came from an external consultancy MM&P.

The Executive and Senior User/*Customer* attended an on site one day seminar which was presented by the external consultant. This provided a good basis for their role but the lack of experience showed on two occasions when they accepted a major change to the project by approving Request For Changes that took the project outside of the Project Brief and Project Initiation Document. Once this had been pointed out they took immediate steps to rectify the situation.

The members of staff allocated to the Project Assurance Function also required training and it was found that they required supplementary help during the project. The role of Configuration Librarian was split between the Project Support Assistant and a member of the Specialist Supplier team this worked well except for a small problem when several Pirate copies of a document were made for a cascade briefing which were inadvertently used as the basis of another Product. The problem arose because the version used was out of date.

Section Two   The involvement of the Project Management Team in the planning and control process.

The majority of the planning effort came from the Specialist Supplier who did ensure that the members of the Project Assurance Function were fully involved in the process of developing and agreeing the Product Descriptions and in providing input to the Checkpoint and Highlight Reports.

The quality of the involvement and advice given by the members of the Project Assurance Function improved as their experience in PRINCE grew. The coaching provided for the members of the Project Assurance Function as part of the ongoing consultancy support helped this confidence to grow.

Project Assurance Function

168

The only real problem came from the member of the Project Assurance Function responsible for User/*Customer* Aspects in Stages 4 and 5 where the volume of work initially overwhelmed the User/*Customer* community until they were allowed to spend additional time on the project.

The estimates provided by the member of the Project Assurance Function responsible for User/*Customer* Aspects were proved to be extremely accurate this I believe was due to the long experience of the person selected for this role.

Section Three   The operation of the Quality Review process.

In Stage 1 and 2 of the project the members of the Project Assurance Function tended to prefer formal Quality Reviews. This was caused by their inexperience, the lack of guidance in when to use what form of review. To counter this problem two actions were taken.

The first was to produce a checklist of the considerations that should be made when deciding between formal and informal reviews. The second was some additional training and coaching in the Quality Review process and conduct of the review meeting.

All scheduled Quality Reviews were held. The quality of the Product Descriptions improved during the later Stages of the project as the Quality Criteria became both realistic and useful to the producer of the Product. This again was due to the inexperience of the Project Management Team but this time I believe it was due to not having used the PRINCE structured project management previously.

Section Four   The operation of the Project Issue Process

There were 31 Project Issues submitted during this project. The majority of these came in the early Stages of the project. The introduction of project information into the regular cascade briefings did reduce the flow of the reports. The only concerns that the procedure gave was that twice the scope of the project seemed to be expanding out of control and the freezing of the User/*Customer* Requirements did help considerably.

Project Assurance Function

169

Section Five   Observations on the project management standards and procedures used.

The major success in this project was the use of the planning and control software. This provided all of the PRINCE planning diagrams and the turnround document system used for telling team members what is to be done and then for submitting actuals saved a considerable amount of effort. The standard proforma for all of the reports proved to be useful and they were only modified so they could be used in the cascade briefings.

The Configuration Management system worked effectively and apart from two isolated incidents involving User/*Customer*s making pirate copies of documents there were no problems.

The allocation of the roles to the individuals was successful although the majority of the appointees had no experience of PRINCE and had not had any training when the job descriptions were agreed.

Section Six   Recommendations for future projects.

The recommendations are:

1.   Training in PRINCE should be undertaken at the outset of the project prior to the discussions about the job descriptions.

2.   When team members are inexperienced then the services of an independent coach/mentor should be provided to help them come to terms with role and the tasks and activities.

3.   A revised standard for plans should be developed which uses the Product Flow Diagram as the main document rather than the Project Plan.

Project Assurance Function

EXAMPLE OF A PROJECT CLOSURE REPORT - PROJECT ASSURANCE FUNCTION

To: The Project Board
                Ace Plumbing Supplies Ltd.

From :   The members of the Project Assurance Function.

Introduction

The stock and sales project has now been completed and this report has been prepared for the Project Board by the members of the Project Assurance Function to provide a summary of the lessons learnt during this project which should be taken into account when further projects are undertaken in the company.

This report is divided into six Sections.

Section One	Selection and appointment of the members of the Project Assurance Function.
Section Two	The involvement of the members of the Project Assurance Function in the planning and control processes.
Section Three	The involvement of the members of the Project Assurance Function in the Quality Review process.
Section Four	The involvement of the members of the Project Assurance Function in the Project Issue Process.
Section Five	The observations of the members of the Project Assurance Function on the project management standards and procedures used.
Section Six	Recommendations for future projects.

Project Assurance Function

171

Section One   Selection and appointment of the members of the Project Assurance Function.

For the members of the Project Assurance Function responsible for Business and User/*Customer* Aspects this was their first experience of operating in a PRINCE project. The selection of the two members of staff to fulfill these roles were we believe correct. When initially selected both of these members of staff were very unsure of the role they were to play in the project and it was not until they had attended the PRINCE Team Members course at MM&P in Bournemouth that they felt able to contribute to the discussion on what their role should be.

Both of these members of the Project Assurance Function felt that during the project it would have been useful to have had the opportunity to discuss their roles and perhaps have some coaching on the skills and techniques required with an independent PRINCE expert. The member of the Project Assurance Function responsible for Specialist Supplier Aspects was a member of the company who developed the system and provided some coaching to the other two members of the team as she had been involved with PRINCE a number of times before. The Project Support Assistant carried out part of the role of Configuration Librarian with the remainder of this role operated by the Specialist Suppliers.

Section Two   Involvement of the members of the Project Assurance Function in the Planning and Control Process.

This aspect of the project did cause some problems due to the inexperience of the members of the Project Assurance Function responsible for Business and User/*Customer* Aspects.

The major problem came with the approval of the Product Descriptions - this was caused by the volume of the documents to be checked and it was not until the member of the Project Assurance Function responsible for User/*Customer* Aspects was granted additional time in the project that this came under control. On the positive side the team were able to suggest that some of the Products originally included in the plans were no longer needed and that overall they did play a full and active role in the planning and control process. The planning and control software used in the project was both easy to use and understand and the PRINCE planning and control documents it produced eliminated a large amount of work.

Project Assurance Function

172

Section Three   Involvement of the members of the Project Assurance Function in the Quality Review process.

This aspect of the project initially gave some problems as the team were not totally confident in what their role was in this process. The on-site training workshop provided by MM&P helped them gain both confidence and experience. The use of the external consultant to help the members of the Project Assurance Function and the reviewers proved to be both valuable and cost beneficial.

Section Four   Involvement of the members of the Project Assurance Function in the Project Issue Reporting Process

The members of the Project Assurance Function were surprised at the number of Project Issue Reports that were raised during the project. They felt initially that this was due to their inability to communicate what the project was all about. This was discussed by the Project Board and the addition of a project progress report into the monthly cascade meetings held for all staff helped to redress this. Towards the end of the project the team felt that they were communicating effectively and that the cascade briefings were probably unnecessary.

The process of evaluation and discussing the Project Issue Reports worked well and did both identify and reinforce the problems identified in the Quality Review process.

Section Five   Observations on the project management standards and procedures.

The project management standards and procedures were defined by the development team and included in the contract that was signed for this project. Generally the standards worked well. The only cause of concern was the complexity of the Stage Plan produced from the planning software however the amendments suggested by the MM&P consultant of having the planning information presented on the Product Flow Diagram rectified this problem. The progress reports and the checklists of Product Delivery and Quality Reviews proved to be extremely useful. The Checkpoint Reports were generated without a meeting and generally this was successful except when on two occasions the input to the planning software was incorrect and the resulting Checkpoint Report was very confusing.

Project Assurance Function

173

Section Six   Recommendations for future projects.

The members of the Project Assurance Function wish the Project Board to consider the following recommendations for future projects.

1. Overview level training in PRINCE should be provided for all members of staff prior to the project starting.

2. Members of the members of the Project Assurance Function should attend both formal training prior to the project commencing and have further top-up training during the project.

3. The members of the Project Assurance Function should be able to call on the services of an independent PRINCE specialist to help them with their role.

4. The input of data to the planning and control software must be double checked by the Project Manager prior to the preparation of any progress reports.

5. A revised standard for plans should be developed which builds on the experience of this project by using as a basis the Product Flow Diagram rather than the Gantt or Bar Chart.

Project Assurance Function

174

EXAMPLE AGENDA FOR END-STAGE ASSESSMENT MEETING

1. Project Manager's Report on the previous Stage.

2. Project Assurance Function Report on the previous Stage.

3. Quality Reviews - Statistics and results.

4. Project Issues - Statistics and results.

5. Standards - project management method and standards.

6. The Project Plan - An update.

7. The Business Case - An update.

8. Risk Assessment and containment strategy - An update.

9. Next Stage Plan and Tolerance.

10. Updates to the Project Initiation Document and approval to proceed.

Project Assurance Function

8   FAULT FINDING

Fault	Action
Do not understand role	Talk to previous member of a Project Assurance Function Read this *Companion* and the detailed notes. Obtain training from an accredited training Supplier. Last resort: Read PRINCE manual.
Organisation complaining about not being involved in the project	The probable cause is insufficient communication on your part. You are not involving the organisation in developing the Product Descriptions, Products, the Quality Reviews or approval of Products. Talk to the relevant member of the Project Board about proposed action.

Project Assurance Function

FAULT	ACTIONS
Product Descriptions inadequate.	Look at previous similar Products. Discuss/contact other User/*Customer*s/members of management. Read guidelines for Products in PRINCE manuals. Seek outside help.
Product Quality Criteria inadequate.	Talk to Team Manager/Project Manager to ensure queries are: - documented - dealt with. Advise the relevant member of the Project Board about the problems.
Products missing from the plans.	Talk to Team Manager/Project Manager and inform the Project Board in writing if the deficiency is not rectified.
Members of the Project Assurance Function not being **allowed** to carry out their role as described in the Project Initiation Document.	Talk/write to the relevant member of the Project Board. They have the authority to settle this matter.

Project Assurance Function

177

9 FORMS/PROFORMA

QUALITY REVIEW INVITATION

Project Name		Project Ref	Stage Name/ No	QR No
To:		From:		Tel:
Product Name			CI No.	Version No.
Venue		Date/Time		Duration
Chairman: Presenter: Scribe: Reviewers:			Tel: Tel: Tel: Tel:	
Attached Documentation:				
Please return QR Question list to: By:				

Project Assurance Function

QUALITY REVIEW QUESTION LIST

Project Name		Project Ref	Stage Name/No	QR No
Project Ref/Name		Reviewer		Tel No
Question No	Location in Document	Description		

Project Assurance Function

QUALITY REVIEW ACTION LIST/RESULT NOTIFICATION

Project Name	Project Ref		Stage Name/No	Q/R No.
Product Ref/Name				Date
Action No	Description	Action By	Target Date	Checked By
Chairman's Sign-off				Date:

Result Notification

Approved - no action required

OK after actions completed

Re-review

Incomplete

Project Assurance Function

CONFIGURATION ITEM DESCRIPTION RECORD

Product Ref	Product Name	CIDR No.					
Product Location	File/Section	PC Directory/Filename					
Product Description Ref/Version	File/Section	PC Directory/Filename					
Quality Review Location	File/Section	PC Directory/Filename					
Product Type	Project Ref/Stage Created	Author/Supplier					
Release Baseline Ref	Linked Product Refs	Security Marking					
Status	Product Description Approved	Work in Progress	Product Draft Available	Product QR Compld	QR Result Note Number	Product Approved	
Date							
	Rework Date						
Version No	Date	QRN/PI RFC/OSR Number					

ISSUE LOG

Version No	Recipient	Purpose	Authority	Issue Date	ExP Date	Return Date	

CONFIGURATION STATUS ACCOUNT

Project Name					Project Reference		Stage Number		
Product Reference	Product Name	Version Number	Author	Status	QRN No.	Date Completed	Location	Linked Products	Comments

Project Assurance Function

182

PROJECT ISSUE

Project Name	Project Ref	Stage No.	PI No.
Author	Date		
Situation Description			
Appraisal			
Affected CI's			
Impact Description			
Recommendation Date:			
Action Date:			
Appraised by: Closed			

Project Assurance Function

183

PROJECT ISSUE LOG

Project Name				Project Ref:			Stage Name/No	
PI No.	Date Raised	Author	CI's Affected	Project Issue Type	Type Change Date	Allocated to:	Date Allocated	Date Closed

Project Assurance Function

184

REQUEST FOR CHANGE

Project Name	Project Ref	RFC No.
Requested By:	Date	From PI No.
Description		
Reasons and Benefits Required Date:		
Supplier Evaluation		
Impact on Project Cost:		

Decision

Approved	Date:	Deferred until:	
Withdrawn		Held for later implementation -	
Rejected		Dependencies	
Authorised by: Role: Date:			

Project Assurance Function

185

CHANGE CONTROL LOG

Project Name			Project Ref			Stage Name/No				
RFC No.	Date Raised	Requester	PI No.	STATUS			DECISION			
				Awaiting Supplier Evaluation	Awaiting Impact Evaluation	Awaiting Decision	Approved	Withdrawn	Rejected	Deferred	Held
				Stage No.						

Project Assurance Function

186

OFF-SPECIFICATION REPORT

Project Name	Project Ref	OSR No.
Requested By:	Date	From PI No.
Off Specification Description		
Reasons and Benefits Required Date:		
Supplier Evaluation		
Impact on Project Cost:		
Decision		
First Reviewed Date: De-scope Date: Deferred to later enhancement	Allocated	

Project Assurance Function

187

OFF-SPECIFICATION LOG

Project Name			Project Ref	Stage Name/No		
OSR No.	Date Raised	Author	PI No.	STATUS		
				Awaiting Impact Analysis	Awaiting Decision	Decision Taken

Project Assurance Function

TECHNICAL FILE - PRODUCT INDEX

Project Name	Project Reference		Stage Reference
Product No	Product Name	File Name	Paper File Reference

Project Assurance Function

189

RISK LOG

| Risk No. | Description | Author | Date Raised. | STATUS | | |
				Awaiting Assessment	Counter or Containment Measure	Owner of the Risk

Project Name · Project Ref · Stage Name/No

Project Assurance Function

190

10   AGENDAS

SAMPLE AGENDA FOR PROJECT START UP METING

1. Confirmation of Project Brief.

2. Confirmation of the Project Management Team Structure, Job Definitions Roles and Responsibilities.

3. Confirmation of the Method of Approach Report

4. Confirmation of draft plan for the Initiation of the Project.

Project Assurance Function

SAMPLE AGENDA FOR FIRST STAGE - AUTHORISATION OF THE PROJECT MEETING

1. Confirmation of Project Initiation Document.

2. Confirmation of the first Stage Plan.

SAMPLE AGENDA FOR MID-STAGE ASSESSMENT - UNPLANNED

1. Explanation of the reason for the Exception Report.

2. Forecast of the impact of the Exception Report on the stage and the project.

3. An explanation of the options to be investigated.

4. Project Manager and Project Assurance Function recommendations.

5. Project Board Decision as to the requirements for an Exception Plan.

Optionally

6. The Exception Plan.

7. Project Board Decision.

8. Action plan for the revision of the Project Brief and Project Initiation Document.

Project Assurance Function

SAMPLE AGENDA FOR END-STAGE ASSESSMENT

1. Project Manager's Report on the previous stage.

2. Project Assurance Function Report on the previous stage.

3. Quality Reviews - Statistics and results.

4. Project Issues Statistics and results.

5. Standards - project management method and standards.

6. The Project Plan - An update.

7. The Business Case - An update.

8. Risk Assessment and containment strategy - An update.

9. Next Stage Plan and Tolerance.

10. Updates to the Project Initiation Document and approval to proceed.

Project Assurance Function

SAMPLE AGENDA FOR PROJECT CLOSURE

1. Project Manager's Project Closure Report.

2. Project Assurance Function Project Closure Report.

3. Confirmation that all the products have been delivered and accepted.

4. Review of Acceptance letters.

5. Review of document and file handover procedures.

6. Review of outstanding Project Issues.

7. Review of outstanding Quality Reviews.

8. Arrangements for the Post Implementation Review.

9. Arrangement for the review of the Security, Backup and Contingency procedures.

Project Assurance Function

195

SAMPLE AGENDA FOR FORMAL QUALITY REVIEW MEETING

1. Chairman's opening remarks and introductions.

2. Author/presenters overview of the product.

3. Reviewers consent to proceed with review.

4. Walk-through of product.

5. Other errors from absent reviewers.

6. Summary of faults found.

7. Follow up action arrangements.

8. Review decision and observations on Product Description and Quality Criteria.

9. Chairman's closing remarks and thanks.

Project Assurance Function